George Hazlitt

Watchmaker's and jeweler's practical hand book

A reliable compendium of valuable receipts and suggestions. Fifth Edition

George Hazlitt

Watchmaker's and jeweler's practical hand book
A reliable compendium of valuable receipts and suggestions. Fifth Edition

ISBN/EAN: 9783337138028

Printed in Europe, USA, Canada, Australia, Japan

Cover: Foto ©Lupo / pixelio.de

More available books at **www.hansebooks.com**

WATCHMAKER'S AND JEWELER'S

PRACTICAL HAND BOOK

A RELIABLE COMPENDIUM OF VALUABLE RECEIPTS AND SUGGESTIONS, CAREFULLY SELECTED FROM PRIVATE FORMULAE, AND THE BEST AUTHORITIES.

EDITED AND COMPILED BY

HENRY G. ABBOTT

Fifth Edition, Revised and Enlarged. 54 Illustrations.

CHICAGO:
GEO. K. HAZLITT & CO., PUBLISHERS,
1892.

COPYRIGHT 1892
BY GEO. K. HAZLITT & CO.

PREFACE.

THE plates of the Watchmakers' and Jewelers' Practical Hand Book having become so worn in the printing of former editions that it has become necessary to consign them to the "waste heap," I decided to improve the opportunity to thoroughly revise the work. Nearly every page has been entirely rewritten and I believe that the work as a whole is a great improvement over former editions. In the matter of illustrations alone a decided improvement will be observed when compared with other editions. All diagram cuts have been discarded and in their place have been substituted photo-engravings made direct from my drawings, which I have aimed to make in their proper proportions. In some instances these illustrations are somewhat smaller than I should have liked them had I the necessary space at my command.

In presenting the following pages I wish to frankly state that I claim no credit for originality; many original ideas will be found in these pages, but the greater part of the matter has been compiled from the best text books of the day, from magazine articles and from suggestions and hints furnished by friends in the trade. The works of Saunier, Grossman, Glasgow, Reid and others have been drawn upon largely for the information here given. My aim has been to supply the student with an elementary work from which he may derive a good insight into the various principles of performing various kinds of work, and at the same time to supply the practical man at the bench with a handy reference work.

My aim has been to present to my readers the most improved processes of doing work, and at the same time to make myself understood, and this information has been compiled from many and various sources. Many of the tools and processes described have been common in watch factory work for many years, but are comparatively unknown to the average watch repairer at the bench. Much of this information has cost the watch factories of the United States thousands of dollars to acquire, through the payment of large salaries and the building of experimental tools and machinery.

With these few remarks the author leaves this little volume to speak for itself and trusts that every reader may find something of value within its covers to compensate him for his time in perusing it and the small outlay in its purchase.

INDEX.

	PAGE.
Adjustment Heater	72
Alcohol Lamp	50
Aluminium	29
Annealing Staff	104
Bench	47
Bezel Chuck	74
Bluing Steel	25
Bow Pens	15
Broaches	56
to Solder	56
Broaching Vertically	56
Bronzes, to Clean	116
Bronzing Steel	25
Broken Screws, to Remove	97
Bushing Wheels	108
to Fit	102
Canon Pinion, to Tighten	105
Cement Chucks	36, 75
Watchmaker's	35
Centering Tool	54
Chalk, to Prepare	113
Chuck, Bezel	74
Jewel	66
Step	83
Wheel	83
Circular Oil Stoves	52
Cleaning Nickel Movements	27

	PAGE
Clocks, Gilt to Clean	113
Copper	25
Curves	13
Cutting Screw Threads	97
Cutters for Screw Head Sinks	67
Cutting Tools, to Sharpen	46
Cylinder Pivots	100
Dials, Silver, to Whiten	95
to Drill	95
to Remove Name from	9
to Remove Stains from	94
Dissolving Soft Solder	33
Douzieme	88
Drawing	9
Drawing Boards	16
Pens	14
Drills and Drilling	90
Drill Rests	65
Drills, to Temper	115
Elevation	9
Eye Glass	37
Files	53
to Clean	54
Filing Block	77

INDEX.

	PAGE.
Filing, Flat	41
Rest	83
Square Holes	44
Fluxes for Soldering	32
Gauge, Douzieme	88
Staff	84
German Silver	28
Gold Solders	31
Springs	93
Graver, Uses of	44
to Sharpen	46
Hairsprings, to Prevent Rust of	94
Hand Tongs	70
Hands, to Fit	95
Hard Solders	30
Hard Steel, to Drill	115
Jewel Chucks	66
Pin Setter	74
Settings to Polish	110
New	110
Lamp, Alcohol	50
Student	50
Lathes	57
Lathe Wax	35
Length of Staff	103
Light and Position	37
Mainspring Winder	71
Marble Cases, to Clean	115

	PAGE.
Nickel	27
to Restore Color of	27
Oil Stones	51
Circular	52
Oil Sinks	97
Parallel Rules	14
Pearls, to Clean	116
to Drill	116
Pinions, Worn, to Remedy	105
Pivots, Cylinder	100
Friction of	101
State of	100
to Polish	99
Pivot Drills	90
Polishers	79
Polishing Steel	23
Wheels	107
Plan	10
Preparing Articles for Soldering	32
Proportional Compasses	15
Protractor	12
Relation of Spring and Barrel	93
Repair Clamps	34
Rose Cutter	112
Rounding-up Attachment	77
Ruby Pins, to Tighten	110
Rust, to Remove	105
Rusting of Steel	24

INDEX.

	PAGE.
Rusty Hairsprings, to Avoid	94
Saw Arbor	79
Screw Head Sink Cutters	67
Tailstock	82
Threads, to Cut	97
Second-Hand Holder	71
Shape of Pivots	100
Show Windows to Prevent Sweating	114
Silver Dials, to Whiten	95
German	28
Solders	31
to Remove Ink Stains from	114
Soft Solders	31
to Dissolve	33
Soldering Clamps	34
Fluxes	32
Stay Springs	33
Tweezers	35
Solders and Soldering	30
Gold	31
Hard	30
Silver	31
Soft	31
Spickerman Cement Chuck	76
Springs, Gold	93
to Soften	93
Staff Gauge	84
Length of	103
to Anneal	104
Stay Spring, to Solder	33
Steel	19
Flat Polish of	23
Hard, to Drill	115
Polishing	23
to Anneal	21
to Bend	20
to Blue	25
to Bronze	25
to Draw Temper from	21
to Protect Against Rust	24
to Restore Burnt	22
to Remove Rust from	24
to Soften	22
to Work	21
Step Chucks	83
Tailstock, Screw	82
Traverse	82
Teeth in Wheels	106
Tempering Drills	115
Tin	26
Tools, to Mark	112
Triangles	13
T Squares	16
Tweezers, Soldering	35
Twist Drills	90
Watch Cases, to Clean	114
Glasses, to Reduce Diameter of	96

INDEX.

	PAGE.
Watch Jewels, to Test	109
Watchmaker's Cement	35
Wheel Chucks	83
Wheels, to Bush	108
Wheels, to Grind	109
to Polish	107
Worn Pinions, to Remedy	105
Zinc	26

WATCHMAKERS' AND JEWELERS'
PRACTICAL HAND BOOK.

PART I.

DRAWING AND DRAWING INSTRUMENTS.

A KNOWLEDGE of arithmetic, geometry and drawing are all essential to the young man who hopes to become proficient in the art of watchmaking, and if he is deficient in knowledge in these branches, the sooner he purchases the necessary text books and starts to master them the better. Saunier very aptly says, that every watchmaker worthy of the name should be able to make and to understand the drawing of a machine or of any horological instrument. Many inventors, and even ordinary workmen, would avoid a large amount of handwork, often useless, and occupying much time, if, instead of at once putting an idea into practice with brass and steel, they were able, as a preliminary, to make for themselves a correct design, drawn to scale. The representation on paper of the side view of an object or its projection on a vertical plane is known as an *elevation*, while the projection on a horizontal plane or a view of the object as seen from above is known as a *plan*. A section is a view of a body as it would appear if cut in two and one portion removed in order to expose the interior. A section is usually indicated by a series of parallel lines drawn close together and at an angle of about 45° to the vertical,

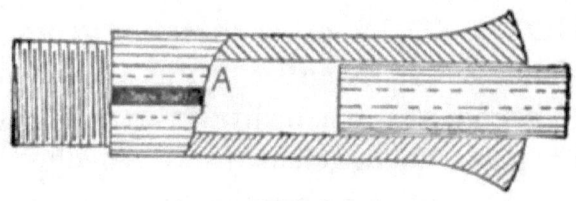

Fig. 1

as shown in Fig. 1. Drawings are sometimes made however, in what is known as diagram style, in which no parallel lines are used in showing a body in section, and interior cavities are represented by dotted lines as shown in Fig. 2. The continuation of the outline of an object which passes behind or into an-

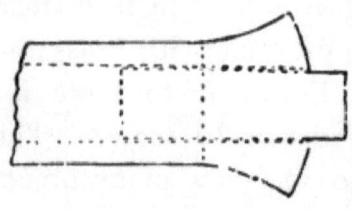

Fig. 2.

other object is usually indicated by dotted lines as shown in Fig. 2. In the shading of projecting objects it is usual to assume that the light falls upon the object from the upper left hand corner of the paper and the same rule is usually followed in indicating depressions or cavities. A glance at Fig.

3 will be sufficient to show that the circle at A represents a hole or cavity, while B indicates the head of a screw. At A the shade falls at the upper left hand side while at B it falls at the lower right hand side. Sometimes in order to show objects which are behind others and in order to convey an idea both of the section and elevation at the same time a piece is represented as broken off, as shown at A, Fig. 1. In other cases objects are shown as broken ff because it is unnecessary to prolong their length or width in order to convey the idea desired, as at the left hand side of Fig. 2 or as is often seen in illustrations of articles having long handles, legs, etc., the handles or legs being represented as broken off.

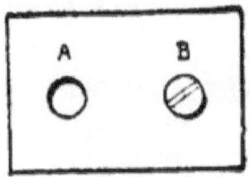

Fig. 3.

A good quality of light weight card-board will be found superior to paper for watchmakers use. The designs should be first drawn lightly with a lead pencil, and then gone over carefully with India ink, after which all remaining traces of the pencil and finger marks, etc., may be removed by means of India rubber or stale bread. A number 4 Faber pencil and prepared liquid India ink, will be found the most convenient and desirable. If you desire, however, you may prepare your own ink by grinding the sticks with water. Drawings made in India ink are permanent, and are not liable to become obliterated by constant handling as are those made with a lead pencil. About all the instruments that a watchmaker will require for his drawings are, a good ruler, a triangle, T-square, a drawing pen, combination compasses, to take bow-pen and pencil, a few crow-quill steel pens, a protractor, a drawing board and some thumb tacks.

There are many other instruments that will be found very useful as you progress, but many of them can be made by the ingenious watchmaker for considerably less than he can purchase them, and at the same time the experience gained in their making will prove valuable to him.

The Protractor. The protractor is made of various substances, horn, hard rubber, celluloid, brass and German silver, and the patterns vary as much as do the materials. Fig. 4 repersents a common form of the instrument. A complete circle consists of 360° and protractors are sometimes made in this form, having a bar across the center for the purpose of indicating the center of the arc. In the style shown in Fig. 4 the arc is divided into 180°, or

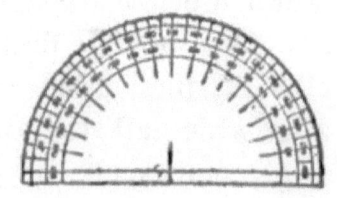

Fig. 4

one-half a circle. The protractor is used for determining and for drawing angles of various degrees. The workman can easily make a good protractor from a piece of sheet brass, but care must be taken in laying out the degrees, and as they can be purchased for 25 cents upward, it is seldom worth while to make them.

Triangles. Triangles similar to Fig. 5, are made in wood, celluloid, hard rubber, German silver and steel. The ingenious workman will do well to make a set of at least three triangles of various sizes and various pitches, say one 45 degrees, as per cut, and one 30 and 60 degrees, and 3, 4 and 6 inches long.

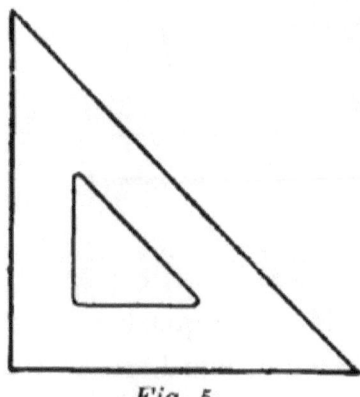

Fig. 5.

Curves. Celluloid, pear wood or hard rubber curves, like those shown in Fig. 6, will also be found very useful by the young draftsman, as with them he can do much better work than he otherwise could. These curves, in all shapes and sizes, may be generally purchased at artists' supply depots.

Fig. 6.

Parallel Rules. In rulers, the parallel is perhaps the best pattern to purchase, as with it you can more easily rule a considerable number of lines truly parallel and also are able to keep them more nearly an equal distance apart. This form of rule is shown in Fig. 7, and from the figure the student can readily

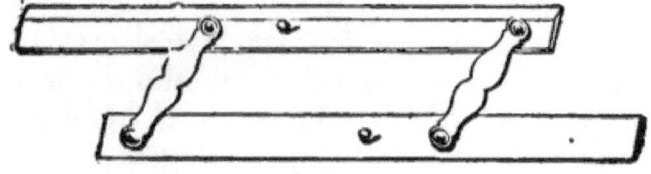

Fig. 7.

infer the method of using it. The T-square is first set against the edge of the drawing board and at the proper place, and the parallel rule is then laid against it, the arms being first separated. After drawing a line the arms are drawn together the required amount to produce the desired space between the lines and another line is drawn. As the rules are connected by swivelled arms, the lines must of necessity be parallel.

Drawing Pens, Etc. The drawing pen, bow pen, combination compasses, etc., are too well known to need description, but for the benefit of the amateur who has no knowledge of these instruments, illustrations are given, Fig. 8 being a bow pen, and Fig. 9 combination compasses. These tools will be all that it is necessary for the amateur draftsman to have in order to make intelligent drawings, but there are many other instruments and devices that will be found useful as you progress in the art. Many of these you can make for yourself, if you are so inclined, as for example the proportional compasses.

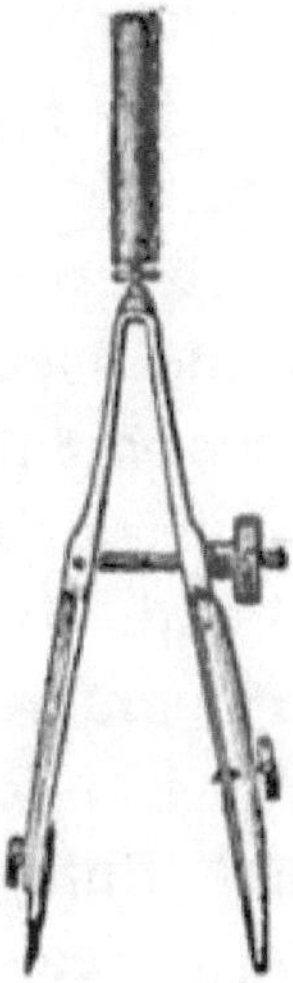

Fig. 8.

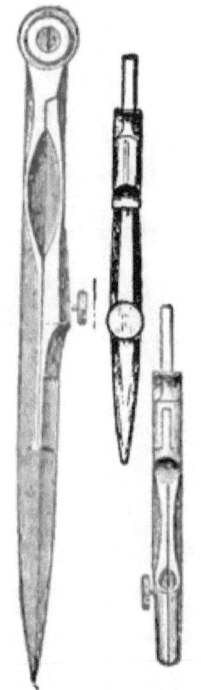

Fig. 9.

Proportional Compasses. These instruments, which are also known under the name of proportional dividers, will be found very useful in making enlarged or reduced drawings in which it is essential to maintain the relative proportions of the original. They consist of two equal legs terminating in points as shown in Fig. 10. The legs are cut through for a portion of their length, and are provided with a slide which acts as a hinge, and which can be clamped in any desired position by means of a set screw.

Graduations are marked upon the edges of the slots so that the legs may be set, so that the upper or smaller ones will measure ½, ⅓, ¼, etc., of the lower ones.

The T-Square. In T-squares, perhaps the best for all round uses is the pattern known as the patent unique square, which is illustrated in Fig. 11, as it combines all the advantages of the ordinary square with fixed head, while it is also very useful for diagonal lining of all kinds. By marking a scale on the edge of your drawing board, and another on the inner edge of the head, similar to the vernier, the distances between lines can be made very accurate and can be brought down as fine as $\frac{1}{25}$ of an inch without trouble.

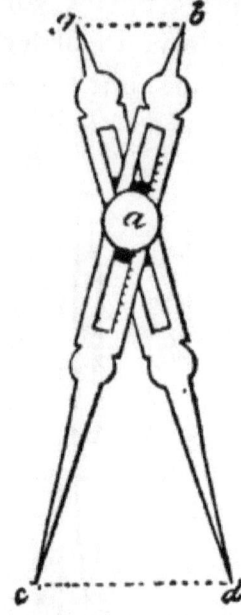

Fig. 10.

Drawing Board. The drawing board should be made of sound, well seasoned wood, preferably pine, as the thumb tacks may be more readily inserted and removed from pine than hardwood, and

Fig. 11.

should be at least 18x22 inches. It should have mortised cleats upon both ends, as shown in Fig. 12, in order to prevent the board from cracking or curl-

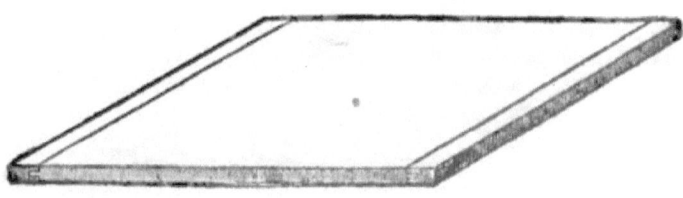

Fig. 12.

ing, and if of large size, all the pieces of the center should be glued with the heart side uppermost, to prevent warping.

The student having provided himself with the above supplies should then purchase an elementary work on mechanical or scale drawing, and with practice he will soon be able to produce creditable drawings of his proposed work.

PART II.

MATERIALS EMPLOYED BY WATCHMAKERS, THEIR TREATMENT AND APPLICATION.

Steel. Steel may be regarded as a compound of iron and carbon, generally speaking; though other substances, such as silicon, etc., may be present in very small quantities. It exhibits a great variety of textures and degrees of hardness, some being very soft, others extremely hard. The crystalline structure also varies greatly; some are fine and close, others are very open, coarse and porous. These qualities fit it for a great number of uses in diversified situations, and it is of the highest importance that the steel used should be adapted to the particular requirements.

The young watchmaker should accustom himself to study the different varieties of steel he is working. He will thus be able to select the proper variety of steel for any particular purpose when called upon to do new work, or to make parts which can not be purchased from material dealers. He should also observe closely the changes taking place during the operations of hardening, annealing and tempering, that he may know how to conduct them properly.

For most horological purposes, such as making pinions, pivots, staffs, etc., cast steel is preferred, because it can be highly polished, turned perfectly round and does not get distorted in smoothing.

Steel for cylinder escapements should be drawn. The reason is that the greater ductility of drawn steel renders it less liable to crack in hardening.

To Bend Tempered Steel. It very frequently happens to the repairer that he desires to bend a spring, but fearing the risk of breaking it, abandons the idea. In such a case the following hint may be useful: Suppose it is desirable to bend a side click spring of a Swiss bridge watch, which, by the way, is generally made of poor steel. Lay hold of the end in which the screw goes with a pair of brass-nosed sliding tongs, holding it in the left hand; then press a piece of brass against the click, bending it in the direction desired, and, at the same time, holding it over the flame of a spirit lamp until the center or spring part becomes a straw or dark red color. This will have the desired effect. The fact that spring-tempered steel is brought to a dark red blue twenty times over, will not reduce it below its former temper; on the contrary, it will tend to equalize and improve the temper and render it less liable to break. Again, suppose a cylinder pivot, or any pivot on any of the escapement parts are bent and you wish to straighten it by this process: Take a small brass bushing, fit it to the pivot and hold over the flame of the lamp, bending it at the same time in the desired direction.

To Anneal Hardened Steel. It may sometimes happen, that hardened steel parts require a few finishing touches, which can not be done because they are too hard and their polish would be ruined by annealing them, because it turns blue, and the piece then requires renewed polish, which consumes a great deal of time. The most practical way then is to cover the steel part with the oily dirt from the oilstone, after which it can be annealed with impunity, that is, the flame is, with the blow-pipe, directed to the point required. The article is afterward cleansed in benzine.

To Work Hard Steel. If steel is rather hard under the hammer, when heated to the proper cherry red, it may be covered with salt and hammered to about the shape desired. More softness can then be obtained, if required to give a further finish to the shape, by sprinkling it with a mixture of salt, blue vitriol, sal-ammoniac, saltpeter and alum, made cherry red again, sprinkled with this mixture, and hammered into shape. This process may be repeated until entirely finished. When ready, the steel is hardened in a solution of the same mixture. This method is recommended by prominent workers.

To Draw Temper From Small Steel Pieces. Place the articles from which you desire to draw the temper into a common iron clock key. Fill around it with brass or iron filings, and then plug up the open end with a steel, iron or brass plug, made to fit closely. Take the handle of the key with your plyers and hold its pipe into the blaze of a lamp until red hot, and then let it cool gradually. When sufficiently cold to handle, remove the plug, and you will find the article with its temper fully drawn, but in all other respects just as it was before. The reason for having the article thus plugged up while passing it through the heating and cooling process, is that springing always results from the action of changeable currents of atmosphere. The temper may be drawn from cylinders, staffs, pinions, or any other delicate pieces by this same method with perfect safety.

To Restore Burnt Steel. Borax, 3 ozs.; sal-ammoniac, 8 ozs; prussiate of potash, 3 ozs.; blue clay, 2 ozs.; resin, ¼ pound; water, 1 gill; alcohol, 1 gill. Put all on the fire and simmer till it dries to a powder. The steel is to be heated, dipped in this powder, and afterward hammered.

To Soften Steel. Heat it brown red, and plunge it in soft water; river water is best. Do not heat over red brown, however,'else it becomes hard when plunged. But if you plunge it as soon as it turns red the steel will be soft enough to cut with ease.

Flat Polish of Steel Work. To polish such parts as rollers and collets, first get a flat surface, by rubbing with fine emery on a glass plate or a bell-metal block, and afterward finish off on a zinc block with diamantine; but for levers, you must use a long, flat bell-metal or zinc polisher, and press the lever into a piece of soft wood (willow is the best) in the vise, moving the polisher instead of the work. For large articles, such as indexes or repeater racks, which are not solid, and spring, it will be found best to wax them on to a small brass block and polish them underhand, in the same manner as rollers.

Polishing Steel. If the steel is of moderately good temper, use a zinc polisher with diamantine; a tin polisher is better for soft steel. The diamantine should be mixed on glass, using a beater, also of glass, with very little watch oil. Diamantine mixed with oil becomes gummy, and quite unfit in a day or two, and turns black, if brought into contact with metal, in mixing.

To Polish Steel. Take crocus of tin oxide, and graduate it in the same way as preparing diamond dust, and apply it to the steel by means of a piece of soft iron or bell-metal, made in proper form, and prepared with flour of emery, same as for pivot burnishers; use the coarsest of the crocus first, and finish off with the finest. To iron or soft steel a better finish may be given by burnishing than can be imparted by the use of polishing powder of any kind whatever. The German method of polishing steel is performed by the use of crocus on a buff wheel. Nothing can exceed the surpassing beauty imparted to steel or even cast iron by this process.

To Remove Rust from Steel. For cleaning purposes, etc., kerosene oil or benzine are probably the best things known. When articles have become pitted by rust, however, these can only be removed by mechanical means, such as scouring with fine powder, or flour of emery and oil, or with very fine emery paper. To prevent steel from rusting, rub it with a mixture of lime and oil, or with mercurial ointment, either of which will be found valuable.

To Protect Steel. After having cleaned the iron or steel article, anoint it with a solution of wax in benzine, using a fine camel's hair brush. By this treatment, articles exposed to acid vapors, may be protected against rusting. Another method is to cover the steel or iron with a layer of a mixture obtained by boiling sulphur with turpentine oil; this evaporates and leaves the sulphur upon the surface as pure sulphur, which again combines with the metal and forms sulphuret of iron, by heating the articles, if small, over a gas or alcohol flame.

To Blue Steel. In order to blue steel pieces evenly, the following will give satisfactory results: First, blue the object without any special regard to uniformity of color. If it proves to be imperfect, take a piece of deadwood that does not crumble too easily, or of clean pith, and whiten the surface with rouge without letting it be too dry. Small pieces thus prepared, if cleaned and blued with care, will assume a very uniform tint.

To Bronze Steel. Methylated spirit, 1 pint; gum shellac, 4 ounces; gum benzoine, ½ ounce. Set the bottle in a warm place, and occasionally agitate. When dissolved, decant the clear part for fine work, and strain the dregs through muslin. Now take 4 ounces powdered bronze green, varying the color with yellow ochre, red ochre and lamp black, as may be desired. Mix the bronze powder with the above varnish in quantities to suit, and apply to the work, after previously cleansing and warming the articles, giving them a second coat, and touching off with gold powder, if required, previous to varnishing.

Copper. The only use made of pure copper in horology is for the construction of compensation pendulums, as wire in electric clocks, and as a base for receiving the enamel for watch dials. It is the only satisfactory metal for this purpose, as its ratio of expansion and contraction is the same as that of the enamel, and consequently the latter will not scale or crack off. Pure copper, although very soft, is difficult to work with the graver or file, as it is so tough that it will throw up a burr instead of coming away with the tool.

Zinc. Zinc, formerly called spelter, is an elementary metallic body of coarse grain, brittle and showing a bluish white color when fractured. It is used in the form of rods for compensating pendulums. It is brittle at $32°$ F, malleable at $200°$ F. and brittle at $400°$ F. It melts at $420°$ F. and burns with a green flame at red heat, forming oxide of zinc. It is annealed in boiling water. Commercial zinc generally contains lead, arsenic and traces of iron, all of which contribute to render it brittle. Pure zinc should not be melted in iron ladles, as it will take up enough iron to injure its malleability; fire clay or plumbago crucibles are generally used when it is desired to keep the metal pure. It shrinks at the moment of crystallization, and hence will not make a sharp casting.

Tin. Tin is a white metal, soft, with a rather coarse and glistening fracture. It is used for making solder and, in the shape of small rods, for polishing with rouge. For this purpose it is much more efficient when pure, or nearly so. The readiest way to judge of its purity is to melt a piece and cast it in a small mold about ¾ of an inch in width or diameter. After melting and pouring, watch the metal while cooling; if pure it will harden perfectly smooth without exhibiting any signs of crystallization at the moment of solidification, while the presence of small quantities of foreign metals causes it to be covered with a network of needlelike crystals, which are the more numerous as the metal is less pure.

Nickel. Nickel is a grayish white metal, about as hard as iron and capable of a high polish. It resists oxidation unless in the presence of moisture, when it forms a reddish oxide. It ranks next to iron in magnetic qualities. It is much used in plating, and also in alloys, with iron, copper, zinc, tin and antimony. By the addition of $\frac{1}{10}$ to $\frac{3}{10}$ of magnesium, or of $\frac{2}{10}$ of phosphorous, nickle becomes malleable and ductile and is rolled into sheets and drawn into wires. It is used for making the plates and cocks for what are known as nickel movements in American watches.

To Restore the Color of Nickle Movements. Take 50 parts of rectified alcohol, 1 part of sulphuric acid, and 1 part nitric acid. Dip the pieces for about 10 to 15 seconds in this composition, then dip them in cold water, and afterwards in rectified alcohol. Dry them with a piece of fine linen, or in sawdust. Nickel and the greater part of those metals liable to tarnish, may be restored to their primitive color by dipping in the following bath: Dissolve in a half a glass of water, 6 or 7 grains of cyanide of potassium; plunge the pieces in this solution and withdraw them immediately. As the cyanide mixes well with water, it is sufficient to rinse them once in the latter to destroy any trace of the cyanide. After this, dip the pieces in alcohol, and dry them in boxwood dust, in order to keep them from rusting. The balance, even together with its spring, can be subjected to this operation without any danger. If the pieces to be restored are greasy, they must be cleaned with benzine before being dipped in the cyanide, because it will not touch grease. Cyanide of potassium, being a violent poison, great care has to be exercised, and the operation should be performed in a well ventilated place. The same bath can be preserved in a bottle, and serves for a long time.

German Silver. German silver is an alloy of copper, nickel and zinc, with an occasional addition of tin. When used in objects that require soldering 2 per cent. of lead is added. When this is the case it is sometimes called silver solder. It has a more yellow appearance than nickel, is softer, finer, and closer; takes a high polish, and does not oxidize readily. It has an extended use in the arts, for fine tools, as mathematical instruments, etc., and was formerly much used as a basis for electro-plated ware, etc. It is also much used in European watch movements, often erroneously termed "nickel" movements. German silver is used only for the plates, cocks and bars, and all holes not jeweled are bushed with brass, as German silver soon blackens and destroys the oil, and the pivots wear sooner than when working in hard brass. For this reason it has not been popular with watchmakers for the cheaper grade of watches, i. e. those without jewels.

Aluminium. This is a white metal, malleable, ductile and capable of a high polish, which tarnishes on long exposure to the air, giving the metal the color of pewter. Its chief use when pure, is in situations where lightness is desired, as it is only one-fourth the weight of silver. This makes it desirable for the hands of large clocks, spectacle bows, and the tubes of telescopes, etc. It has an extensive use in alloys; an alloy of 90 parts copper and 10 parts of aluminium is malleable, ductile, and resists wear to such an extent that it is much used for boxes of lathes and other parts of fine tools. It is used for lever escape wheels, and some other parts of watches, and also, on account of its golden color, for the cases of cheap watches, but the latter always tarnish where not subject to daily wear. It also has an extensive use in cheap jewelry, under the name of oreide, Roman gold, etc.

Solders and Soldering. A solder is an alloy employed to unite, by means of heat, two metallic bodies placed in contact. To do this, a solder must be more fusible than the metals it unites, otherwise the latter would be damaged by the heat used to melt the solder. In the event of soldering a piece of work which requires several solderings at or near the same place, the last alloy used will require to be considerably more fusible than the first, or otherwise the heat would be so great that the earlier joints would melt.

Solders are commonly divided into two groups, known respectively as hard and soft solders. The former fuse only at a red heat, while the latter fuse at low degrees of heat. The following table shows the composition of various hard solders which have stood a practical test for various purposes:

Description.	Parts Brass.	Parts Zinc.	Parts Tin.
Refractory	4.00	1.00	
Readily Fusible	5.00	4.00	
Half White	12.00	5.00	1.00
White	40.00	2.00	8.00
Very Ductile	78.25	17.25	

Gold solders should approach the articles to be soldered in both color and fusibility as nearly as possible. The following gold solders are in general use:

Description.	Parts Gold.	Parts Silver.	Parts Copper.
Hard Solder for 750 fine	9.0	2.0	1.0
Soft Solder for 750 fine	12.0	7.0	3.0
Solder for 583 fine	3.0	2.0	1.0
Solder for less than 583 fine,	2.0	2.0	

The following hard silver solders have been thoroughly tested:

Description.	Parts Fine Silver.	Parts Copper.	Parts Brass.	Parts Zinc.
First	4		3	
Second	2		1	
Third	19	1	10	
Fourth	57	28.6		14.3

The soft solder most frequently used consists of 2 parts of tin and 1 of lead. The following table gives the composition of various soft solders with their respective melting points:

No.	Parts Tin.	Parts Lead.	Melts at Deg. F.	No.	Parts Tin.	Parts Lead.	Melts at Deg. F.
1	1	25	558	7	1½	1	334
2	1	10	541	8	2	1	340
3	1	5	511	9	3	1	356
4	1	3	482	10	4	1	365
5	1	2	441	11	5	1	378
6	1	1	37	12	6	1	380

Soldering Fluxes. As a soldering flux for hard solder, use borax rubbed to a paste with water on a slate. For soft soldering, dissolve a small piece of zinc in pure hydrochloric acid until effervescence ceases. After twenty-four hours remove the undissolved zinc, filter the solution, add one-third its volume of spirits of sal-ammoniac and dilute with rain water. This fluid is non corrosive. Where two smooth surfaces are to be joined together, you can make an excellent joint, by moistening with the fluid and then having placed a small sheet of bright looking lead which comes as a lining for tea boxes between them, pressing firmly together, hold over your lamp until the lead melts. The closest kind of a joint can be made in this way.

Preparing Articles for Soldering. The thorough cleansing of surfaces to be joined is of the utmost importance but more especially so in the case of soft soldering. This cleansing may be effected by means of acids or by scraping with a knife or graver. In soldering, it is frequently necessary to hold the parts in position by means of binding wire, which is made of soft iron, or the parts may be retained in position by means of many of the clamps now sold for that purpose. The blow pipe is used most extensively for watchmakers' work though small soldering irons are sometimes employed. Articles are usually placed upon a piece of charcoal while soldering, but when soldering gold or silver an asbestos block or piece of pumice stone will be found more desirable. Char coal emits gases while under the blow pipe which enter into the alloy of gold or silver and render them brittle.

To Solder a Stay Spring. Stay or lifting springs are often broken, and the watchmaker has frequently none of the right size nor the time to make a new one. In such a predicament he can mend the old one and have it just as good as new, by placing the broken parts together and binding them firmly to a piece of coal, then soldering them with 18-karat gold. It requires a strong heat and plenty of borax; then finish off, nicely harden and temper in the usual manner.

To Dissolve Soft Solder. Nitric acid may be used safely for gold not lower than 12 k. and is very effective. The following is suitable for all grades of gold and silver: Green copperas 2 oz., saltpeter 1 oz., reduced to a powder and boiled in 10 oz. of water. It will become crystalized on cooling. Dissolve these crystals by the addition of 8 parts of spirits of salts to each part of crystals, using an earthenware vessel. Add 4 parts of boiling water, keep the mixture hot and immerse the article to be operated upon and the solder will be entirely removed without injuring the works.

Soldering Clamps. The Magic Repair Clamps,

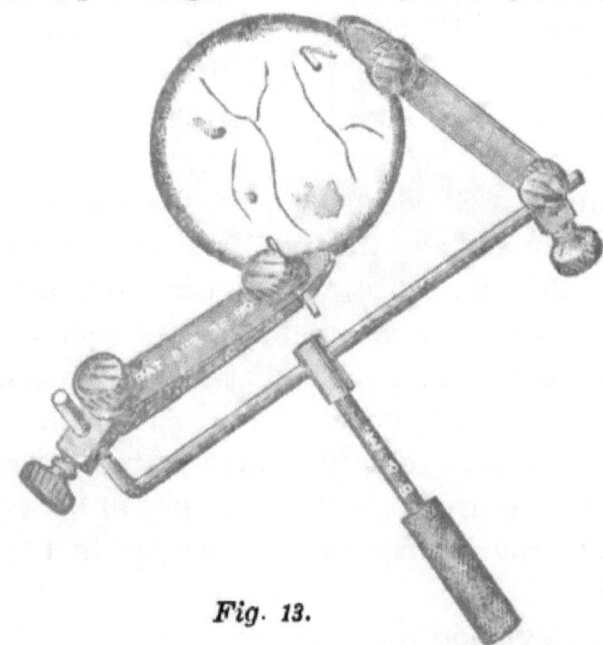

Fig. 13.

shown in Fig. 13, will be found very useful for holding various kinds of work while soldering. In the illustration, one of the clamps is shown holding the dial in position while the foot is held by the other clamp in the position in which it is to be soldered. This tool is so arranged that the end screws and handle may be used as feet so that the tool with the work in it will stand up, thus leaving the operator free to use asbestos block or charcoal in one hand and

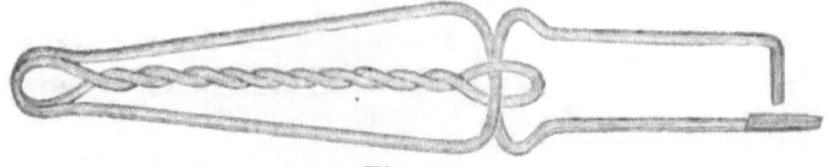

Fig. 14.

the blow pipe in the other. The number of positions in which this tool can be placed and also its uses are almost limitless. Soldering tweezers, similar to those shown in Fig. 14, will also be found very useful for holding small work while soldering. They may be obtained from material dealers generally.

Watchmakers' Cement. The best lathe cement, or wax, which is kept for sale by all dealers in tools and materials is prepared in the following way. Eight ounces of the best gum shellac are thoroughly incorporated with one-half ounce of ultramarine blue. The shellac is first dissolved in a small quantity of water over a sand or water-bath and the ultramarine added gradually. This makes the strongest and best wax for use on cement brasses or chucks.

Mode of Applying Lathe Wax. In applying wax in the lathe it is essential that the wax chuck or cement brass be thoroughly freed from all old and burnt cement. On the face of cement chucks or brasses will be seen a series of concentric circles cut with a graver, as shown in Fig. 15. These circles are cut to increase the adhesion of the cement. Do not allow them to be filled up with old burnt cement. It is of the utmost importance that the chuck be brought to the right heat before the wax is applied. If wax is applied to a cold chuck it will not hold firmly and is very liable to scale off while you are in the act of performing a very important part of the work. Keep the chuck revolving in the lathe while heating and also while applying the wax. Apply as little wax as possible between the object and the chuck. If you apply a thick layer, the object will lose its rigidity. Hold the object against the face of the chuck by means of a pegwood supported on the T rest. After centering to position remove the lamp and allow the chuck to revolve until the wax sets.

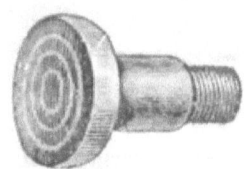

Fig. 15.

PART III.

LIGHT AND POSITON.

The preservation of the health is most important, as it exercises an important influence on the keenness of the sight and the steadiness of the hand, two of the chief requirements of a workman. Good habits contracted in youth are sometimes difficult to keep up, but when the watchmaker has tried them long enough to be convinced of their influence on his health, and consequently on his work, he will appreciate them sufficiently to keep them up.

The Glass. No watchmaker should use a glass that is not truly acromatic. If, on looking at any bright object, rings of colored light appear in the glass or a fringe of colored light around the object, the glass should be rejected as unfit for use. If compelled to use a glass of this nature take a small brush and some black, lusterless paint and paint a ring around the inside of the lens, commencing at the frame and gradually working toward the center until the colors disappear. Or a ring may be cut out of paper, blackened and put inside the frame next the lens. This will diminish the field of view, but it will be much easier on the eye. Do not use glasses of too great power, as they needlessly tire the eye. It is well to have several glasses of different powers, and to use the weakest ones as much as possible, reserving the stronger glasses for use only on the most delicate operations. The glass should not be held in position by contracting the muscles of the eye for more than a moment or two. A glass holder can be made of twisted wire, or an old mainspring can be riveted on the frame of the glass so that it will maintain the glass steadily in any position with no susceptible pressure. A few holes should be drilled in the frame of the glass near the eye, to ventilate it and thus avoid the irritation caused by the heating of the enclosed air and the deposition of moisture on the inner surface of the lens.

It is a good practice to habituate yourself to using either eye with the glass. In many delicate operations this will frequently allow a much easier position of the body than if but one eye were used.

Light. The watchmaker should use a window facing north whenever possible, as the light from the north is more evenly diffused; shadows are not cast by it; reflections do not bother the operator, and a given finish on any metal will always have the same appearance. Consequently the operator can work more rapidly and with less fatigue than when he is working by a changeable light, as is always the case where the sun strikes the bench for a portion of the day. If much bothered by sunlight striking the polished metal, an engraver's glass screen may be used. This is a large double convex bottle, mounted in a frame so as to be easily adjusted to any position. This is filled with water slightly tinged with aniline blue, and the yellow rays of the sunlight, passing through the blue become changed to green, which is a restful color and does not annoy the eye. A very slight amount of blue is sufficient. Others use a muslin curtain strongly blued in washing, and some varnish the window glass with a colorless varnish containing a slight admixture of blue. It will seldom be found necessary to resort to these methods, however, unless compelled to work in extremely unfavorable situations.

Position when working. Do not use a stool with a stuffed seat, as it frequently causes irritation by pressure on the prostatic gland. A stool with a cane, wood, or leather top will be found much better than one with a soft cushion. The top should be large enough to allow a frequent change of position. It should have an adjusting screw to enable the workman to change the height at will, thus avoiding compression of the muscles of the chest and neck during any long and tedious operation. An old piano stool with a broad seat, covered with calfskin tightly strained over the upholstery, so as to harden it, makes a very good stool and can be purchased cheaply. By thus providing himself with the means of changing his position easily and frequently, the workman will avoid cramping of the legs, chest and neck, irritation at the base of the spine, backache, and various other ills arise from improper positions in working; and by being careful to sit as erectly as possible, round shoulders, and much strain on the eyes will be avoided.

PART IV.

MANIPULATION.

It is very essential that the novice should first learn to file flat and square, to turn round and to hammer a piece of metal without deteriorating it. In the modern training of an apprentice these accomplishments are too often neglected, principally owing to the shortness of the time he can afford to devote to learning his trade.

To File Flat and Square. It is a common practice to set an apprentice to work with an old file and a piece of iron. This is a mistake. The apprentice will do better to start with a round piece of hard wood, dressing it down to a square, first with a rasp and finishing with a new bastard file. He should not leave hard wood until he can file a surface so well, that, on placing a metal rule across its surface in any direction, it is found to be flat. When he can do this he can safely advance a step and work upon brass. Avoid rapid movement and excessive pressure and take care that little or no pressure is applied during the backward stroke. Avoid short and jerky movements. No written instructions can replace those of a competent teacher.

Do not be afraid of using new files in the above practice as the wear will not injure them but rather bring them into good condition for working iron or steel.

When filing an object which is held on a cork or wood block fixed in a vise, and one hand only is used for filing, special care should be taken to lay the file flat without any hesitation after each return stroke, and the hand should be able to feel if the file is in this respect and to at once bring it flat.

Mechanical Devices for Filing Flat. There are many mechanical devices for filing flat but the two examples here shown are among the best. Let it be supposed that we desire to finish up the square on a fusee or a barrel arbor; you will naturally find some difficulty in filing the sides of the square flat, if you proceed in the ordinary manner. Now we will suppose you have a dead-center lathe; place your arbor

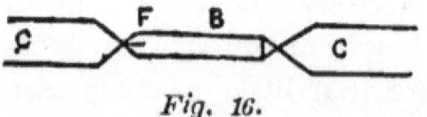

Fig. 16.

between the dead-centers, allowing it no end-play, but perfect freedom to revolve. Now, if we have in the first place, made a flat on the sides, we may apply the file to the surface when swinging between centers with perfect impunity, and be assured that the surface will follow the direction of the file or burnisher as the case may be. The two centers, C, are supposed to be fixed in their respective places, while the arbor, B, is free to revolve, and the square, F, can be finished up with perfectly flat sides. The file being applied to the flat, F, the freedom of motion will enable the article to meet it at any position the file may take. In polishing, the value of this little tool will become more apparent, for you have doubtless noticed, that though you may have filed a surface flat, it will almost invariably round up in polishing. When small, thin work is to be done, that will not admit of swinging between centers like an arbor, the following attachment may be used.

Fig. 17.

This cradle, as it were, which is made of brass, acts in the same manner as does the arbor when swung between the centers. Shellac the pieces to be filed on the cradle, S, and proceed the same as with the arbor. Let the holes for the centers be deep enough to prevent the cradle from dropping out during the filing process. Work can be filed, stoned and finally polished without removing from the cradle.

The workman may make the cradle of any size and length to accommodate the dimensions of the pieces he wishes to work on, and as it is so easily made he may have a number of different sizes and and depths. In planting the centers on which it is to vibrate, it must be taken into consideration that the nearer the line of the centers the surface to be worked, the truer will be the work, as it will vibrate much more easily than when the surface falls below the center.

Filing Square Holes. To file a square hole it is necessary to reverse the work very often; a square file should first be used, and the holes finished with either a diamond-shaped file or a half-round. This leaves the corners square, as they properly should be.

Use of the Graver. Just as in working with the file, advice and demonstration by a good master are here indispensable. The materials should be worked in the same order as explained under filing, i. e., hard wood, brass, iron and steel. The apprentice should turn exclusively with the point of a square or lozenge-shaped graver. This is the only possible method of learning to turn true, and it enables the workman to acquire a great delicacy of touch.

At Fig. 18, three styles of gravers are shown, but the one marked B is the most applicable for use of apprentices. Avoid gravers of the shape of C until such time as you have thoroughly mastered the art. The graver shown as A is applicable for all ordinary work on the lathe.

Much depends upon the condition of your gravers and the manner of using them. It is of the utmost importance that they be kept sharp, and as soon as they begin to show the slightest sign of losing their keenness, you should sharpen them, otherwise you will be inclined to use pressure, which will soon render the hand heavy. Two ways of holding the graver are shown in Fig. 19. If the graver is applied to the work as shown at A, it will cut a clean shaving, while if applied as shown at B it will ruin the point of the graver without materially forwarding the work. Holding the graver as shown at A also has other advantages. The force of the cut, when the graver is held in this position, is towards the hand holding it, and should it catch from any cause the jar of the obstruction will be conveyed immediately to the hand, and it will naturally give, and no harm will be

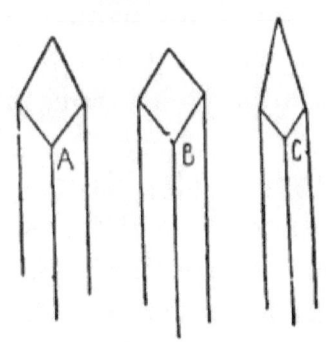

Fig. 18.

done. If, on the other hand, the graver should meet with an obstruction while held in the position indicated at B, the force of the shock will be in the direction of the rest, downward, as shown by the arrow, and the rest being rigid and unyielding, the result will be disastrous not only to the graver but to the work also. Do not attempt to remove much material at a time, but rather aim to see how small a shaving can be made. In this way you will acquire a delicacy of touch that will prove valuable to you in after life.

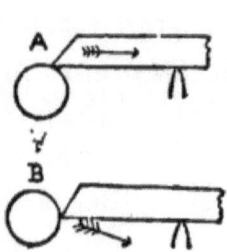

Fig. 19.

Lubricant for Sharpening Cutting Tools. Instead of oil, which thickens and makes the stone dirty, use glycerine as a lubricant when sharpening your gravers. The cutting surface of a graver and the amount of pressure exercised on the stone while sharpening being small, it is necessary to employ glycerine almost pure or with one or two drops of alcohol. The proportions of the lubricant vary according to the instrument operated on. An article with a large surface sharpens best with a limpid liquid, as three parts of glycerine to one part of alcohol. Kerosene oil is the best thing to use as a lubricant for hard stones such as the Arkansas.

PART V.

TOOLS AND APPLIANCES.

The Bench. Watchmakers' benches of various patterns, both open and curtain-top, may be purchased ready-made from almost any material dealer. The curtain or roller-top benches possess many advantages over the ordinary open-top benches, but the cost sometimes debars their purchase. With a curtain-top bench the work may all be left upon the bench at night, the side raised and the curtain dropped and the top and all the drawers, containing tools, are locked automatically, thus preventing any meddling with tools or work and excluding all dust. The bench shown in Fig. 20 is one of the latest designs on the market, the points claimed for it being that it is raised sufficiently from the ground to allow sweeping under it, and its extreme lightness. The frame is made of iron, and is similar to those used for sewing machines. The foot wheel is fastened to the iron frame on the left, instead of being supported by uprights from the floor. For the benefit of those who wish to have their bench made by a local carpenter or cabinetmaker a design is submitted, at Fig. 21. This bench is made of black walnut, veneered with French walnut and bird's eye maple. The top

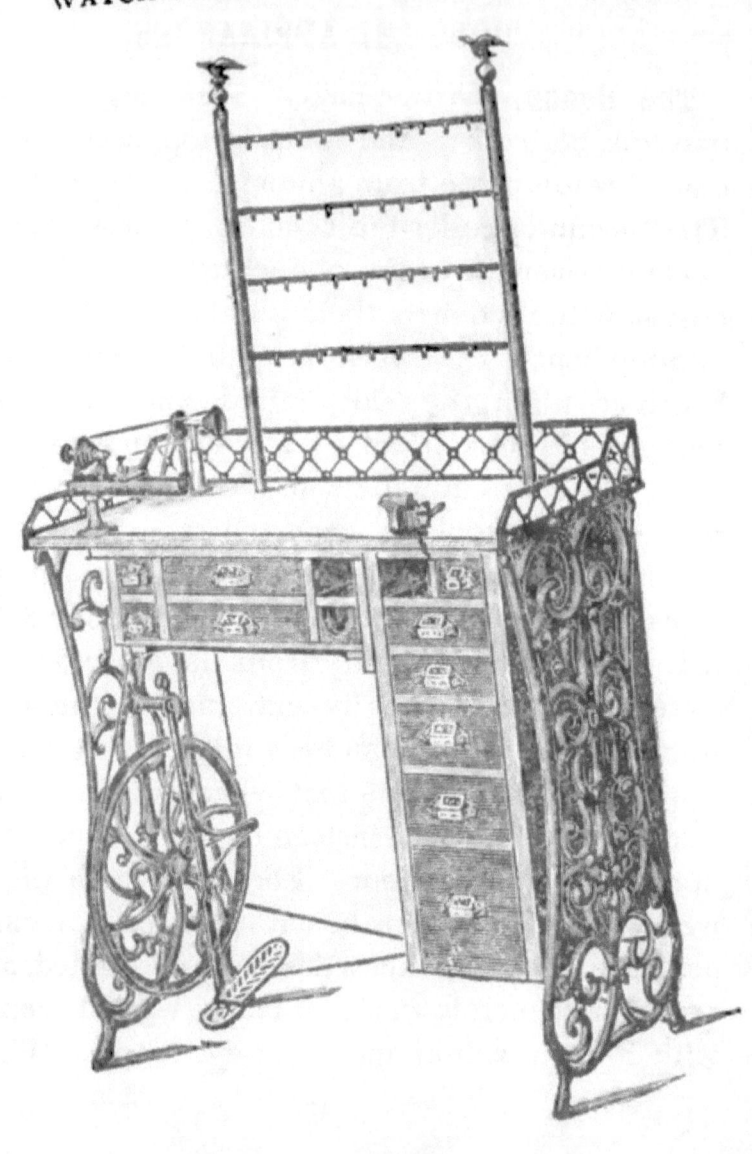

Fig. 20.

is 21 inches wide by 41 long, and is 33 inches high. The drawers on the right hand side are ten inches wide. In the center are two drawers, and the left

Fig. 21.

hand side is entirely boxed in. The lathe wheel weighs 40 pounds, and the space in which it runs is only five inches wide. Use a walking motion treadle.

Well seasoned black walnut, cherry or red cedar are the best woods for a bench. From this sketch any first-class cabinet maker should be able to make a good bench. The little square pin attached to the right hand end of the bench is a Carter patent pegwood cutter, which is made fast to the bench by screws, and dispenses with the use of a bench knife to sharpen pegwood; this little tool is a grooved plane with a steel cutter that sharpens the pegwood very nicely and quickly, and only requires the use of one hand.

The Lighting. For night work or during dark days where a light is necessary, perhaps nothing will be found superior to what is known as the student lamp. This lamp is fitted with an Argand burner and uses kerosene oil. If gas is used an Argand burner will be found the most desirable. Where possible, either on gas or oil lamps, use a duplex glass shade, which is dark green on the outside and white on the inside. This pattern shade throws all the light directly on the bench, and shades the eyes from the glare. Do not raise the lamp too high, but rather have it at such a height that your eyes are in the shade while the work is well in the light.

The Alcohol Lamp. The simplicity lamp, shown in Fig. 22, is a favorite one with American watchmakers. It has nine facets on the font, and it can readily be adjusted to any required position. Care should be exercised that the wicks of alcohol lamps are not too tight, and the interior and exterior should

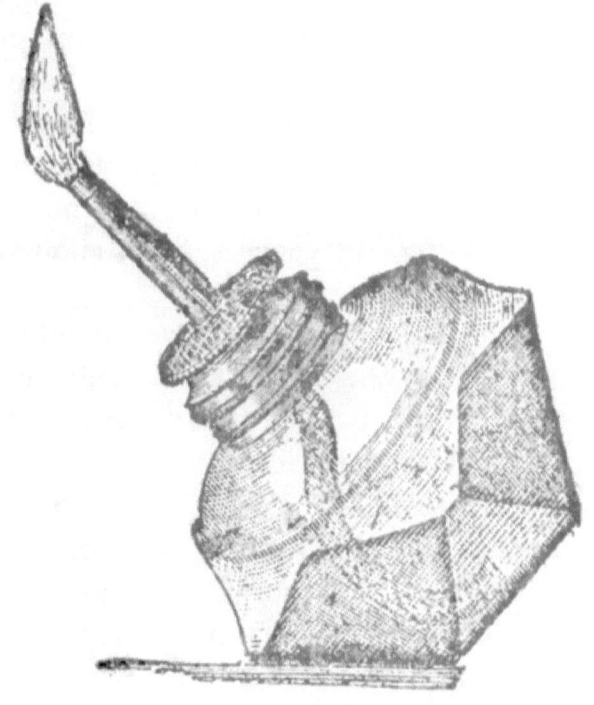

Fig. 22.

be kept free from dirt. The wick should be kept long enough to reach well down into the alcohol and the font must not be filled too full.

Oil Stones. It is well to have at least two good oil stones, one rather soft and coarse for first grinding to shape, and another, say a Turkey stone, for the final edge. The lubricant for oil stones has already been referred to on page 46. Should the surface of your oil stones become ridged through irregular wear, the level may be restored by rubbing the stone on a smooth board covered with a paste of fine sand or emery and water. Should the stones become saturated with oil or their surfaces become impaired owing to the gumming of the lubricant, they should be put into a bath of strong lye or benzine and allowed to remain two or three days, and the oil will be eaten out.

Circular Oil Stones. Circular oil stones will be found much superior to the ordinary flat oil stones commonly used, for sharpening drills, gravers and other cutting tools, where it is desirable to have an exact angle. An Arkansas or Turkey stone dressed down to circular form, and say $1\frac{1}{2}$ inches in diameter, when mounted for the lathe will be found to be superior to the ordinary flat stones. Apply the lubricant to the stone the same as you would to a flat one, and hold your graver or drill at the exact angle you want the cutting edges to be, and turn at moderate speed. Truer angles and better work can be produced in this manner than by any other. Emery or corundum wheels mounted in a similar manner, will be found very handy accessories to the watchmakers' bench. The wheels may be obtained from material dealers or dental supply houses, in sizes varying from ½ x ⅛ to 3½ x ¾ inches. A set of three or more will prove very valuable for grinding dials, to allow freedom of motion for wheels, when fitting new dials; for grinding milling

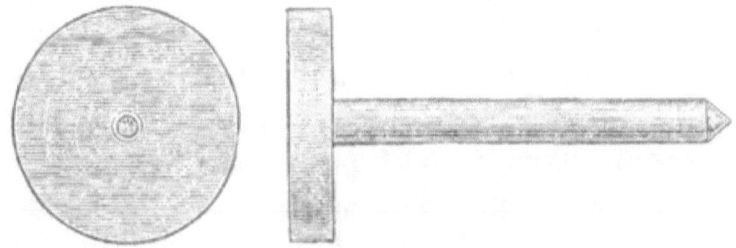

Fig. 23.

cutters, drills, gravers, etc. When purchased these wheels have a central hole, and they can be mounted for use by the watchmaker in the following manner: Turn down a piece of No. 30 Stubbs steel wire, to the size of the opening in your wheel, and rivet the wheel firmly upon it as indicated in Fig. 23. The best sizes for watchmakers' use are ½ inch, 1 inch and 1½ inch in diameter.

Files. A new file should never be used on steel; it is better to use it for a while on brass, handling it carefully. A file that has been properly used and has passed from brass to steel will last four or five times as long as one that has been used on steel when new. If a new file be employed upon steel, or if sharp quick strokes are made, the cutting edges of the file will chip off and the hard particles will be embedded in the metal operated upon, injuring both file and work.

To Clean Old Files. Old files that are clogged with dirt, grease and metal can be restored by boiling for half to three-quarters of an hour in a solution of 4 ounces of saleratus to a quart of water. After boiling, rinse in clean cold water, and then place them in a solution composed of 4 ounces of sulphuric acid to a quart of water. The small files should be removed at the end of thirty minutes, but larger ones may remain in for two or three hours. After removal from the bath wash in clean water and brush with a stiff brush until dry, then oil thoroughly to prevent rusting.

Centering Tool. This tool is very easily made and will save much time. Every workman knows how much time is spent in centering up in the universal head. To be sure there is a needle or point which plays through the hole in the chuck, but it is very hard to center accurately by it. Of course, if the work is not particular, the needle will do, but where it is essential that the work should be accurately centered, the needle fails. To center with this tool, unscrew your rest and remove it, then place the shaft, c fig. 24, in rest holder and adjust it till the needle point R

touches the top of hole as shown at A. The index
hand will then note the variations as the head revolves. If the wheel is too low, the index will point
above center and vice versa. By gently tapping, the
wheel can be accurately centered, which will be de-
noted by the index hand remaining motionless at E.
The body of this indicator is made of sheet brass and

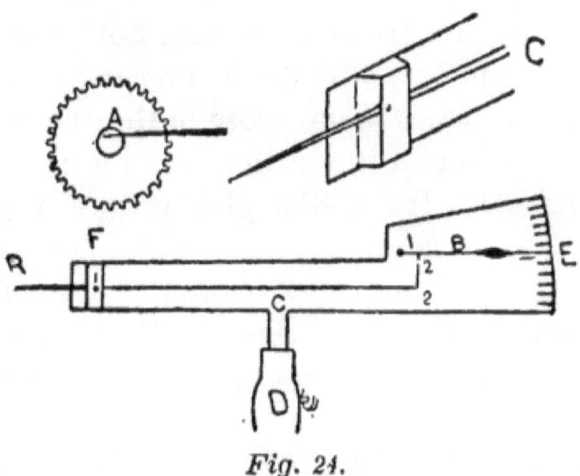

Fig. 24.

should be about five inches long by two inches in
width at the larger end. The shank, c, is made to
fit in rest holder and is either riveted or soldered to
the body; R is steel or copper wire sharpened to a
fine point and balances on a pivot at 1; B is an old
clock hand pivoted to the body at 1; 2 and 2 are
pivot joints only and do not go through the body;
C will, perhaps, give a better idea of the end F.

Broaches. Care should be taken to see that the handles of your broaches are properly fitted so that they revolve truly. To test this, rest the points against the fingers of one hand and causing the handle to rotate by two fingers of the other hand, the broach itself should appear to remain true. Sealing-wax answers the purpose as a handle for broaches very nicely, and the broach can be centered in it without trouble. In the latter case hold the broach between two fingers with the handle end downward, and rotate it while held close to the flame of an alcohol lamp so that the sealing wax forms a regular oblong handle. It is well to gently draw a piece of iron charged with rouge along the edges of pivot broaches in order to remove the thread of metal from them. Minute particles of this thread might otherwise remain in the holes, and occasion wear of the pivots.

To Solder Broken Broaches. Steel broaches and other tools are soldered by cleaning well the parts broken, then dipping them into a solution of sulphate of copper, and soldering them with ordinary soft solder. The joint is a good one and will stand ordinary hard wear.

To Broach a Hole Vertically. It is quite a serious thing for young watchmakers to broach a hole vertically; a hole in a plate, for instance, that in a barrel, is seldom maintained at right angles to the surface, when they have occasion to employ a broach. They may be certain of success, however, by adopting the following method: Take a cork of a diameter rather less than that of the barrel or other object operated upon, and make a hole in the length of the cork through which the broach can be passed When the cork has turned quite true on its end and edge, the broach is passed through, and used to enlarge the hole; by pressing against the back of the cock, it is kept against the barrel, whereby the broach is maintained in a vertical position.

The Lathe. The various forms of lathes on the market are so well known that a description of them is unnecessary. Those who contemplate buying a lathe, however, will do well to avoid all cheap imitations of the genuine American article. The American lathe has proved very popular not only at home but abroad, and their popularity has induced many manufacturers in foreign countries to manufacture lathes on the lines of the American pattern. Many of these imitations are inferior both in material and workmanship, their greatest defect being their untruth. These foreign makers send these lathes out guaranteed "as good as the American," and it is not long before the purchaser regrets the fact that he tried to save a dollar or two by buying them. There are six or seven manufacturers of genuine American lathes, and if an untrue lathe by any possibility is allowed to escape the inspector and finds its way upon the market, the American manufacturer is only too glad to exchange it for a perfect article, for his reputation is at stake; but who are you going back upon in case one of these imitation lathes prove untrue and thoroughly unreliable? Above all things purchase a good lathe. Investigate the merits and claims of the leading manufacturers of the genuine article, and then use your best judgment in the selection. The best lathe that money can buy is none too good for the watchmaker. The quality of the work done and the satisfaction which the lathe gives to its owner, depends greatly upon the care which he bestows upon it, providing that originally it was a first-class article.

The American lathe of to-day is a marvel of completeness in its parts, and how many hours, yea months, of study and experiment have been bestowed upon it by its projectors and makers to acquire these points of utility and excellency. What a vast amount of care has been exercised for the production of a perfect lathe. Must this care cease on the moment the lathe passes into the hands of the watchmaker?

It is a very easy matter at any time to wipe off the dust and oil that may accumulate, but does this alone constitute due care? There may be a nice glass case to cover it and keep off the dust, and a very good idea it is if faithfully used; but if a counter shaft is on the bench, or much lathe work is to be done, it soon falls into blissful desuetude, or finishes its usefulness by being broken. Then, often, a cloth is wrapped about the lathe, which soon gets soiled and looks badly, let alone the poor protection it affords.

Dust is omnipresent and the greatest enemy to all active machinery; it insiduously makes its way into every crease and crevice, and if not promptly removed will cause untold damage. We can not get rid of it and must (like the industrious housewife) wage a constant warfare against it.

The care necessary to be given to a fine lathe differs from most other tools; it is not confined alone to the removal of dust and keeping clean, but the fitting properly of the several parts as used. There should be no overstraining when tightening screws, chucks, etc., or when fitting articles in both wire and wheel, and so on through the list.

The face of the lathe bed when it comes from the makers, is (or should be) perfectly true from end to end, in order that head and tail stocks will meet on a direct line of centers, even should they be changed end for end, and a good lathe will meet those requirements. Now, it is obvious to any thinking mind that if this face becomes injured by neglect, whereby the nickling is removed in spots or portions, they will, in all probability, become rusty; this rust will then eat away and throw off more, and soon the face presents an uneven surface, which will tend to destroy the line of centers between head and tail stocks.

The head stock, usually occupying one position, causes less wear at this point or place, while the hand rest and tail stock are constantly being shifted, so where there is more motion or action there must be more wear, especially if dust, chips or grit be allowed to accumulate beneath them, and though the wear is seemingly imperceptible it nevertheless is there and will sooner or later manifest itself, and this is a signal that the level of the bed is becoming impaired and, necessarily, the truth. Thus too much care and attention can not be exercised in guarding against chips and dust when sliding hand rest forth and back on the bed.

At the end of bed, where the tail stock takes position, many watchmakers have the tail stock off, and this portion is more exposed to atmospheric action, also receiving perspiration from the hands when they come in contact. Again, others let the tail stock remain in position, only removing when it comes in the way. In the former case, it is well to devise some means for the protection of bed; this is easily done by making a sheath of chamois skin to slip tightly over the bed; it can be removed and replaced readily, and when it becomes soiled can be washed.

This sheath should be fully two-thirds the length of bed, or reaching from tail end up to hand rest when it is close to head stock. It preserves the bed from dampness, which is considerable in some climates, also the perspiration of the hand and flying chips and dust. In the second case, if the tail stock is allowed to remain on lathe, or, if removed and placed on the bench, it is subjected to all the evils the bed is in the former. Our opinion is, the tail stock should be kept in its compartment in a tight fitting drawer, away from dust and accidental knocks of other tools on the bench; the tail spindle not being nickled, is more liable to rust if left exposed, and should be kept wrapped in a sheath of oiled paper. This may seem superfluous and too much bother, yet it is taking proper care which tells in the end.

The bottom of tail stock should always be brushed off before placing in position, not only for its protection but for fear some particle of grit may be adhering, thereby throwing it out of truth, and screwing it down tight only adds injury to the lathe if allowed to remain.

The head stock demands close attention; the spindle should run freely without end shake, and about once a week should be speeded, meanwhile administering oil until it leaves the bearings clean, and then wiped off. A little oil should be added every day. See that the mouth of the spindle is kept bright and clean; thrust a strip of cloth clear through spindle every now and then, that all dust and dirt may be removed.

Wire and wheel chucks should often be washed in gasoline to remove gummy dirt and oil which is constantly adhering, and it is even well each time a chuck is used, to wash off first, then wipe dry. A little dirt on mouth of spindle, or on chuck, often throws it out of truth, and consequently the article fastened therein also.

When fitting head or tail stock, or in fact any attachment, do so carefully. Do not bang it in place as if you held a grudge against it, and when in position see they are tightly screwed in place.

Having too much end shake on live spindle, especially in soft lathes, causes uneven wear in its bearings, besides not being reliable for true pivoting or any such work.

When the cost of a lathe is taken into consideration, it goes to prove that it is not easily replaced. Where is the jeweler with a stock of goods who would retire without first seeing his valuables were in the safe, but how many are there who think of giving this protection to their lathes? Some do, but the greater per cent. do not. It is a "pious plan" to see that the head stock, tail stock, and attachments are in the safe, and should a fire break out that endangers the store, and no chance to save it, the feeling of satisfaction is great to know the lathe is safe, that is, the more expensive parts, for the bed can be purchased at a nominal cost compared to the attachments.

A word about chuck blocks or stands. The best kind are those made to fit in a drawer of the bench and the holes sunk deep enough to let the chuck (wire) drop full length or to the head, the hole being countersunk to admit the bevel portion. They can easily be picked out with the finger nail. Have the block thoroughly soaked with oil.

To prevent rusting of tools, and especially if the bed shows signs of rust spots, here is a good old remedy: procure some blue ointment, spread it on a cloth and rub the tools or lathe briskly, then wipe off with a clean cloth, wipe dry. This ointment leaves a thin coating of mercury which prevents the action of dampness on the tools. This cure need not be resorted to oftener than once a month, and keep ointment away from gold cases and watch movements. If you find your lathe bed has got in such a condition as to destroy its truth, send it at once to the makers and have it put in first-class condition. Do not trust it, for the sake of saving a little, to some unresponsible firm for repairs.

An excellent lathe for the heavier work of jewelers and watchmakers, such as cannot be performed with

Fig. 25.

satisfaction on the watchmaker's lathe, is manufactured by the W. F. & John Barnes Co., Rockford, Ill., and is known as their No. 5 lathe. This lathe, which is a very popular one with watchmakers, is illustrated at Fig. 25. For screw cutting, the manufacture of watchmakers' tools, fishing reels, tower clocks, and in fact, any of the heavier work which the watchmaker may wish to perform, this lathe is admirably fitted.

Drill Rests. Drill rests will be found very convenient adjuncts to the lathe, and the watchmaker should make a half-dozen of different sizes, from ¼ to 1 inch in diameter, varying by ⅛ of an inch. To make them, use hard rolled sheet brass, a trifle thicker than 1-16 inch; saw out the number you want, a trifle large, so each piece of brass will be ¼, ⅜, ½, ⅝, ¾, ⅞, and 1 inch in diameter, when turned off. Place a steel taper plug in the chuck of your lathe, and turn down a recess, leaving a shoulder on the taper; drill a hole through one of the brass

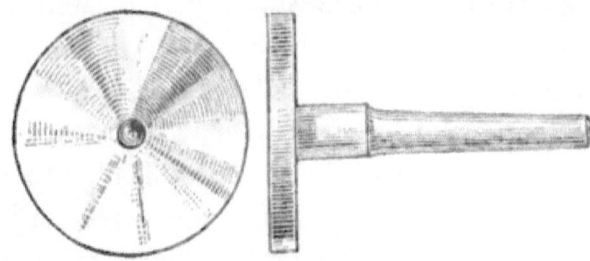

Fig. 26.

pieces already made, to fit the steel taper tightly, and remove from the lathe. Place the end of the taper on a lead block, proceed to rivet the brass on the steel taper tightly and true, replace the taper in the lathe chuck and proceed to turn the face and edge of the brass perfectly true and of the proper size. Proceed the same with all the sizes until the whole set is complete. Every watchmaker knows how hard it is to hold an article to a drill in a lathe and drill a hole perfectly straight. By using a drill rest this may be easily accomplished, by placing the rest in the spindle of the tail stock and placing the article flat against the rest. Loosen the screw on the tail stock spindle and gently move the article against the drill, and the whole will be perfectly upright and all danger of breaking drills will be avoided. Fig. 26 shows a front and side view of these very useful little attachments, which all watchmakers should have.

Jewel Chucks. Jewel chucks, or jewel cement chucks as they are sometimes called, will also be found very useful, and any watchmaker can make a supply of them during his leisure moments. They should be made of brass and threaded to screw into the taper screw chuck of lathe and similar to Fig. 27 in shape. Ten or twelve different sized faces will make a good assortment to select from. They will be found very valuable for fitting odd-sized jewels. Once in a while you will find it impossible to select from your supply of jewels one that will fit the pivot properly, and at the same time fit in the recess in the cock or potance. Select a jewel that fits the pivot, and if the brass setting is too large select one of these jewel chucks that is a trifle smaller than the recess in the potance. Cement the jewel to the end of the jewel chuck, bring to a dead center on the lathe, by means of a peg-wood, inserting it in the hole in the jewel, and as soon as the cement is cool you can proceed to turn down the brass setting to fit the potance. Cement the jewel with the flat side toward the chuck, so that in case the setting is too thick it also can be turned down to the exact thickness of the original jewel's setting. With a full set of these jewel chucks you will be able to utilize many odds and ends and fit a jewel perfectly in a short time, while otherwise you might be compelled to wait several days for the receipt of a jewel from some material house, and then find when it comes that it is not just what you wanted.

Fig. 27.

Screw Head Sink Cutters. These little tools, like the ones just described, can be made by any ingenious watchmaker, and they will be found well worth the time and labor bestowed upon them. Very often a watch is brought in that has a broken end-stone or cap jewel. The jewel is set in a brass setting and is held in place by two screws on opposite sides, the screw heads being let in or sunk even with the surface, and half of the screw head projects over on the end stone. The end stones which are purchased from the material houses are not sunk from these screw heads, but are just as left by the jewel lathe; and when they are fitted into position they fill up one-half of the space left for the screw heads. Now many watchmakers use a graver or small rat-tailed file to cut out these recesses for the screw heads, and the natural consequence is that the job is a bungling one when finished. A set of screw head sink cutters like that shown in Fig. 28 will do this work on the various movements, and do it as well as it is done in the factories. With a set of six, to fit the various makes of American watches, you will be able to do your work in a first-class manner. Select a piece of Stubb's steel wire of the proper diameter for the sized cutter you

Fig. 28.

require, and about one inch in length. Place it in a wire or split chuck in your lathe, and turn one end to a center. Now reverse the wire in your chuck, being very careful that it is centered, and selecting a drill that will pass through the screw hole in the cock, proceed to drill a hole in the center of the wire, and in the flat end, making it about one-sixteenth of an inch deep. Remove from the lathe and with a sharp file or graver, proceed to cut a series of teeth, like those in the rose cutter, as equal and as even as possible. Use a good strong glass for this work, and be sure you have every tooth sharp and perfect, as upon this depends the quick and nice work that you expect from the tool. Now proceed to temper it and give the outside a nice polish. Select a nice piece of pivot wire, of a size that will nearly fit into the hole in the end of the tool, and polish it down to a size to fit snugly into the hole and drive it home. Cut off this wire, allowing about one-sixteenth of an inch to project in the form of a pivot. Taper and polish this pivot and your tool is ready for use. You can now select an end-stone of a diameter to fit tightly into the cock or potance, as may be required, and first placing the hole jewel in position, proceed to press the end-stone tightly against the hole jewel. Now place a sink cutter of the proper size in a split chuck in your lathe and select a medium-sized drill-rest, (see fig. 26), and place it in the tail stock spindle. Hold the cock or potance, with the hole and cap jewel in place as described, against the drill rest, and proceed to run the lathe at a moderate speed and slowly feed the cock or potance to the cutter in the lathe. The projecting pivot in the end of the cutter will pass through the screw hole and be a guide to keep the cutter in the center of the hole. Be careful and do not cut the recess too deep, as these little cutters are deceiving and cut much faster than you think, if you have never used them before. If the projecting pivot on the cutter is well polished it will not injure the thread in the hole in the least.

Hand Tongs. The sliding tongs generally used by the trade for holding minute hands while filing or broaching the hole large enough to fit the cannon pinion, are poor, awkward tools for the purpose. Fig. 29 illustrates a form of hand tongs that will be found very convenient for this purpose, and which

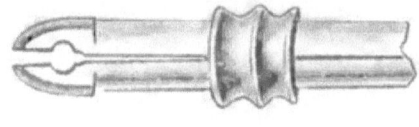

Fig. 29.

can be made in a very little time. Almost every watchmaker has an old sliding pin vise, that is perhaps well worn out and which can be readily converted into a useful tool. If you have no such tool handy you can buy a new one for twenty-five cents and alter it over. Slide the ferrule towards the end tight, and file or saw a slot in the end, about one-thirty-second of an inch wide, and up to the hole that is usually drilled through the sliding pin vise. When this is done, proceed to saw or cut three narrow grooves, lengthwise, on the inside of the jaws of the vise, and of a width and depth sufficient to hold a minute hand securely. The grooves should be similar to those made in the common sliding tongs, and are used in the same manner. Make the slots of three different widths, to accommodate the different widths of watch hands. The tool is operated in the same manner as the sliding tongs, and in fact is simply a modification of that tool. At Fig. 30 a second-hand holder is shown, with a hand in position ready to broach. In order to broach out a new

Fig. 30.

hand, where the boss of the old hand has been preserved, place a small slip of cork upon the end of the broach and insert it in the old hand as far as it will go, and the new hand may then be broached until the cork is reached, before trying it for a fit.

Mainspring Winders. The Stark patent winder, shown in Fig. 31, is a very superior tool, is simple and durable, and should last for a lifetime. The winder is fastened in the vise, the adjustable nut is then turned until the barrel will fit loosely over the jaws, the barrel is then removed and the spring wound on the arbor inside the jaws. Now let the handle turn backward until the arbor is free from the center, pull the arbor back and turn it half round, place the barrel back again over the jaws and spring, and hold it up tightly against the face of the winder with the left hand, at the same time push the arbor forward with the right hand until the barrel and spring are free from the jaws, and the spring will be found in its proper place without further operation. There are two sizes of winding arbors, one for small and

Fig. 31.

the other for large barrels. The arbors are easily changed by turning the thumb screw up until it is free, then changing the arbors and screwing the thumb screw down again.

Adjustment Heater. The Simpson heater, shown in Fig. 32, will be found invaluable when adjusting movements to temperature. The variation of temperature in this heater is one and one-half degrees in twenty-four hours. It is designed to be heated by gas, the cost of heating being but about three cents in twenty-four hours. A small lamp can be used if the watchmaker has no gas at command.

Fig. 32.

Jewel Pin Setter. Fig. 33 illustrates the Logan patent. It is an excellent tool and will save the workman considerable time and much annoyance by its use. Every watchmaker is aware what a difficult and tedious matter it is to set a jewel pin correctly. With this tool the job is accomplished quickly and accurately.

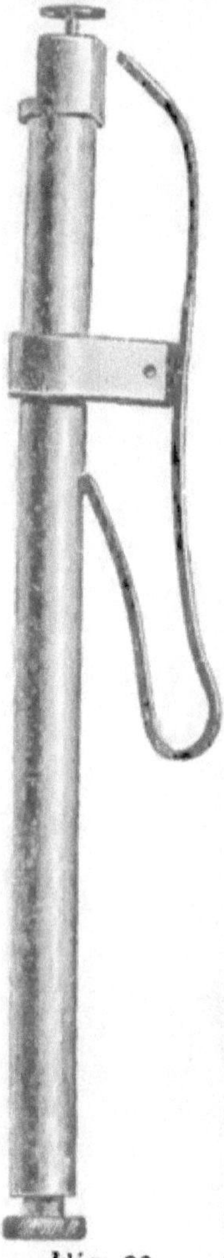

Bezel Chuck. The Snyder Patent Bezel Chuck, shown in Fig. 34, was originally intended for holding bezels only, but it is now made so that it will hold watch plates, coins, etc, and is adjustable to any size. It can be fitted to any lathe and requires very little practice to use it, as it is extremely simple, and any one who uses a lathe can make or repair bezels in a workmanlike manner. It holds the work as in a vise, and no amount of turning or jarring will loosen the jaws, while it may be opened and closed instantly by simply turning the milled nut behind the face plate, thus enabling the operator to turn and fit a bezel perfectly by trying on the case as many times as is necessary. It holds the bezel by either groove, so

Fig. 33.

that the recess may be turned out when too shallow or too small for the glass, or the bezel may be inverted and turned away when it rests too hard on the dial. It will be found especially useful in turning out the inevitable lump of solder from the recess in the bezel, after soldering and in fitting to case, as the process of soldering generally makes the bezel shorter, and consequently it will not fit on the case. It also renders the operation of polishing bezels after soldering, but a few minutes work. In turning out the recess for glass in bezels, especially heavy nickel bezels, it will prove a friend indeed, when for instance, you look through your stock of flat glasses and find none to fit, but have one that is just too large. All watchmakers know that if the groove in the bezel is imperfect it is apt to break the glass. The chuck is also useful as a barrel closer, holding work while engraving, and many other uses that will present themselves to the watch or case repairer.

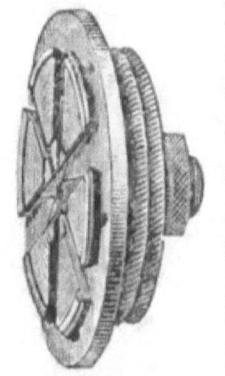

Fig. 34.

Cement Chuck. The Spickerman patent cement chuck, shown in Fig. 35, is a very handy device, as it holds and centers accurately any wheel in a watch while drilling, polishing or fitting new staffs or pinions and all danger of injuring wheels is obviated.

It fits all kinds of American or Swiss lathes. The holder shown in Fig. 36 at *a*, is turned down to nearly the size of the screw for the lathe and the screw cut so the holder will set as close as possible to the lathe. The face of the holder is then turned perfectly true.

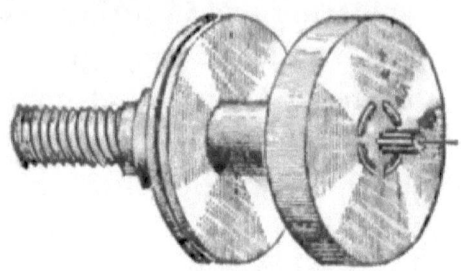

Fig. 35.

Put wheel to be centered in cap *c*, as near to center as convenient and screw on *b*. Then place cement face of chuck *b* against face of holder *a* on the lathe,

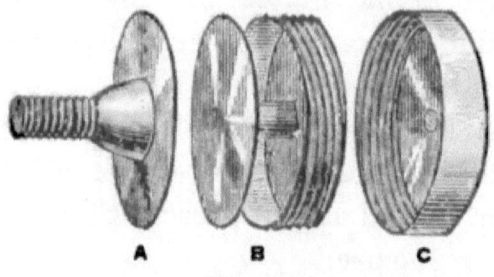

Fig. 36.

and with a lamp, warm the cement between the surfaces, holding the chuck with a stick against the pivot of wheel in the cap, and it will move to an exact center as soon as warmed sufficiently. New cement should be added occasionally between the surfaces, as it hardens and burns away and does not center as well as when new. Fig. 35 shows chuck with wheel inside ready for drilling.

Filing Block. A contrivance made to take the place of the filing rest, which was made of boxwood or bone. It consists of a cylinder of hardened steel which revolves upon a staff which in turn enters a split socket. The surface of the steel cylinder is

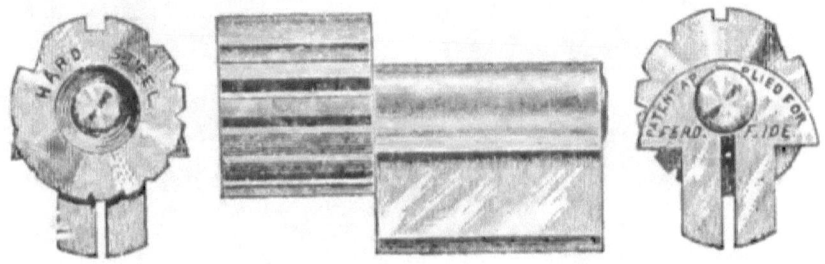

Fig. 37.

grooved with various sizes of grooves for the different sizes of wire, or to suit any work, as shown in Fig. 37. The cylinder is revolved until the desired size groove is brought uppermost, when the split socket is placed between the jaws of a vise, and the vise closed, thus holding the cylinder in the desired position. Fig. 37 illustrates Mr. Ide's patent block which is well made and of superior material.

Rounding Up Attachment. The Webster rounding up tool attachment, shown in Fig. 38, is a very useful adjunct to the lathe. It is attached to the top of the slide-rest. To operate, a pointed taper in the taper chuck is put in the lathe spindle. The wheel to be rounded up is put into the fixture and the wheel adjusted vertically so that the point of the lathe

Fig. 38.

center will be at the center of the thickness of the wheel, after which the lower spindle of the fixture should not be moved. Now remove the wheel, also the taper chuck, and put the saw arbor, with the rounding up cutter, in the lathe spindle, and adjust the longitudinal slide of the slide-rest so that the rounding up cutter will be back of and in line with the center of the rounding up fixture, after which the longitudinal slide of the slide-rest should not be moved. Now put the wheel and supporting collet in place, and proceed with the rounding up.

Saw Arbor. The saw arbor or chuck, as shown in Fig. 39, is made with a projection turned to receive

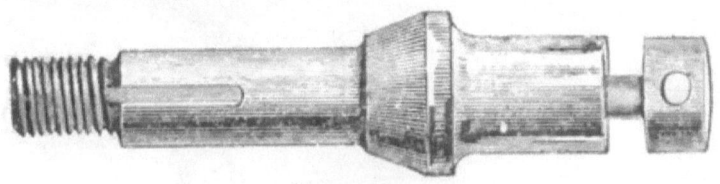

Fig. 39.

a saw, diamond, or emery lap, etc. They are manufactured by the various lathe manufacturers, though the patterns vary somewhat from the illustration here shown.

Pivot Polisher. The pivot polisher is used for grinding and polishing conical and straight pivots and shoulders. It is also useful for drilling, polishing or snailing steel wheels, milling out odd places in plate or bridge where only a part of a circle is to be removed, etc. The circular base being graduated to degrees, it can be set at any angle. The spindle has a taper hole for drill chucks, which makes the fixture very useful for drilling either in the center or eccentric, and by using the graduations on the pulley of the headstock an accurately spaced circle of holes may be drilled. Fig. 40 is the Rivett pattern.

The polisher is used as follows: After the pivot is turned to proper shape, put on your polisher (spindle

Fig. 40.

parallel with lathe bed), with lap back of pivot. Use cast-iron lap first. (Square corners for square shoulders, and round corners for conical.) Lap for conical shoulder can be readily cornered with a fine file, and cross-grind with fine oil stone to remove any lines made by graver. Lines on end can be removed same way, or with slips rubbed on piece of ground glass which has on it a paste of oil stone and oil well mixed.

This will rapidly bring them up to a sharp corner nicer than by the graver. On the iron laps use No.

1 crocus or very fine oil stone powder, well ground down in oil to a paste. When roughened out to your liking, wipe off the crocus, and with a little oil touch the pivot gently; repeat the second time. Then change lap for one of boxwood, and use crocus No. 4, very fine and well ground down to paste. Proceed as with first lap, being careful at all times to keep

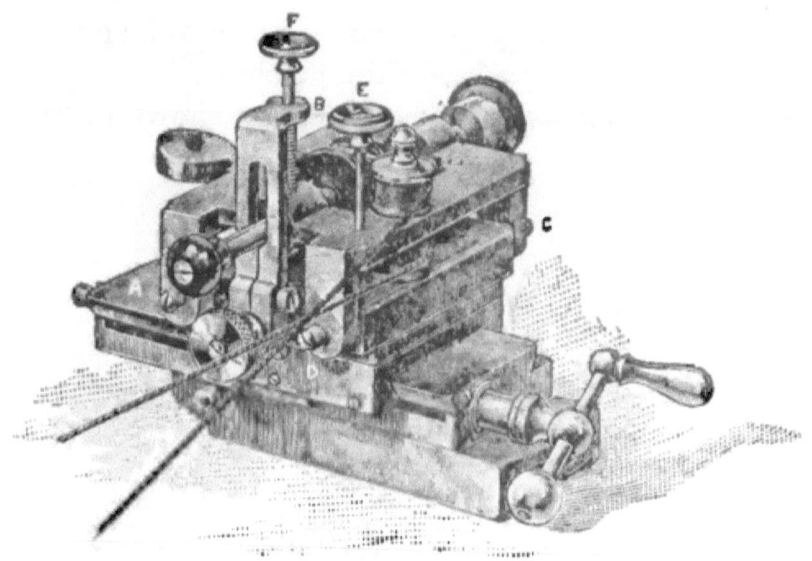

Fig. 41.

the lap properly oiled and not pressed too hard against the work, particularly in the last operation. Also be sparing of your grinding or polishing materials. About three specks of polish with point of a small knife is sufficient. Bring the lap up carefully against the work until spread all the way around, then proceed, bearing in mind that grinding is not polishing, and that to polish nicely the work and lap must be very nearly the right shape. To thoroughly clean the laps, dip in benzine.

Fig. 41 is the Johanson combined pivot polisher, milling and damaskeening machine. For use as a pivot polisher, it will fit any American lathe hand rest or can be used on slide rest. Cutters and polishing laps are furnished with the machine.

Screw Tailstock. This attachment shown in Fig.

Fig. 42.

42, is very convenient for heavy drilling, the spindle being moved by a screw with hand wheel attached.

Traverse Spindle Tailstock. This attachment will be found very convenient for straight drilling. Where the watchmaker has a great deal of drilling to do he will find this attachment invaluable.

Filing Fixture or Rest. These rests will be found very convenient in squaring winding arbors, center, squares, etc. There are several makes of these tools, but they are all built upon the same principle, that of two hardened steel rollers on which the file rests, and Fig. 43 is a fair example. One pattern is made to fit in the hand rest after the T is removed, while the other is attached to the bed of the lathe in the same manner as the slide rest. The piece to be squared is held in the split or spring chuck in the lathe, and the index on the pulley is used to divide the square correctly. Any article can be filed to a perfect square, hexagon or octagon, as may be desired. The arm carrying the rollers can be raised or lowered as required for adjustment to work of various sizes.

Fig. 43.

Step or Wheel Chucks. These chucks are usually made in sets of five, each chuck having nine steps, giving forty-five different sizes. These chucks are very useful in holding mainspring barrels, to fit in the cap of the barrel, should it become out of true.

They are also valuable in trueing up barrels of English lever watches, that are damaged owing to the breakage of a mainspring. They are also very useful

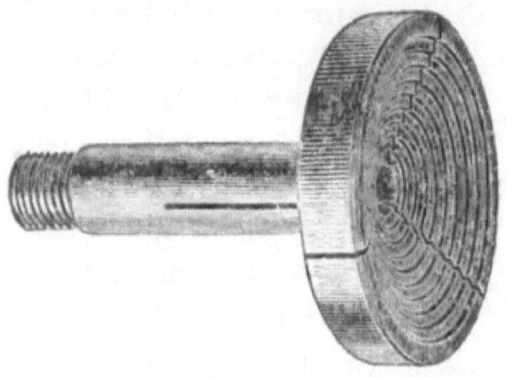

Fig. 44.

in holding almost any wheel in a watch, but particularly convenient in fitting a center wheel to a pinion, or in making sure that the hole in the wheel is in the center. These chucks are made by the various lathe manufacturers and are all similar to Fig. 44, and will hold wheels from .5 to 2.16.

Staff or Cylinder Height Gauge. The obvious advantage of this tool, which is shown at Fig. 45, is the automatic transfer of the measurement so that it may be readily applied to the work in hand. The tool, as the illustration shows, consists of a brass tube terminating in a cone-shaped piece. To the bottom of this cone is attached a disc through which a needle plays. Around the upper end of the tube is a collar upon which is fixed a curved steel index finger. A similar jaw, which is free to move, works in a slot in the tube. The movable jaw is tapped and is propelled by a screw that terminates in the needle point. This tool is very useful in making the necessary measurements required in putting in a staff. To use it in this work, set the pivot of the gauge through the foot hole, and upon the end-stone project the needle such a distance as you wish the shoulder to be formed above the point of the pivot. Next set the gauge in the foot hole as before, and elevate the disc to a height that shall be right for the roller, which is done by having the lever in place, the little disc showing exactly where the roller should come. Finish the staff up to that point, then take the next measurement from the end-stone to where the shoulder should be, for the balance to rest upon. This point being marked, the staff can be reversed and measurement commenced from the upper end-stone, by which to finish the upper end of

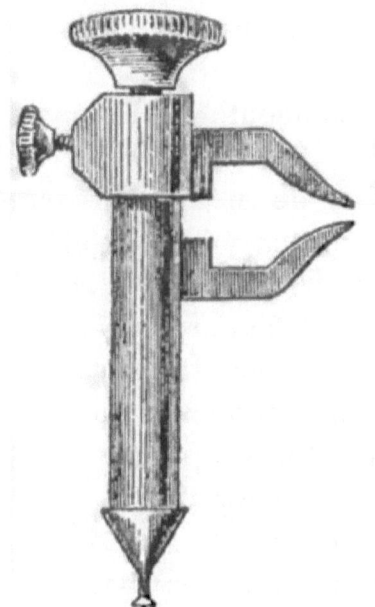

Fig. 45.

the staff. Distances between the shoulders for pinions and arbors can be obtained with the same facility, a little practice being requisite.

Staff Gauge. The tool shown in Fig. 46, the invention of Mr. E. Beeton, is designed for measuring the height of the balance staff from the balance seat to the end of the top pivot. The illustration is enlarged to give more distinctness.

$E\ E'$ is a piece of curved steel about $\frac{1}{20}$ of an inch thick, and $\frac{1}{15}$ of an inch wide. On the lower side fro E' to the end the arm is filed down in width and thickness to correspond to an ordinary balance arm; C is a slot in the upper arm E, which allows A, B, D, A' to be moved backward and forward. $D\ D'$ is a round brass post drilled and tapped; the part D' has a thread cut on it, and the part shown in the slot C fits with easy friction. B is a locknut, drilled and tapped to fit the thread on D'. It is for the purpose of clamping $D\ D'$ against the arm E. $A\ A'$ is a small steel screw with milled head, and is made to fit the tapped hole in $D\ D'$.

Mr. Beeton describes his method of using this tool as follows: Take your measurement of the distance, *the balance seat is to be from the end of the top pivot*, as follows: remove the end stone in balance cock, and screw the cock on the top plate, (18-size full plate movement) then taking the plate in your left hand,

and tool in your right, place *H* in position, so that the end of the screw *A'* rests on the jewel in the balance cock, and notice the position of the arm *E'* which corresponds to the balance arm, between the top plate and under side of balance cock. If the distance between the arm *E'* and end of screw *A'* is

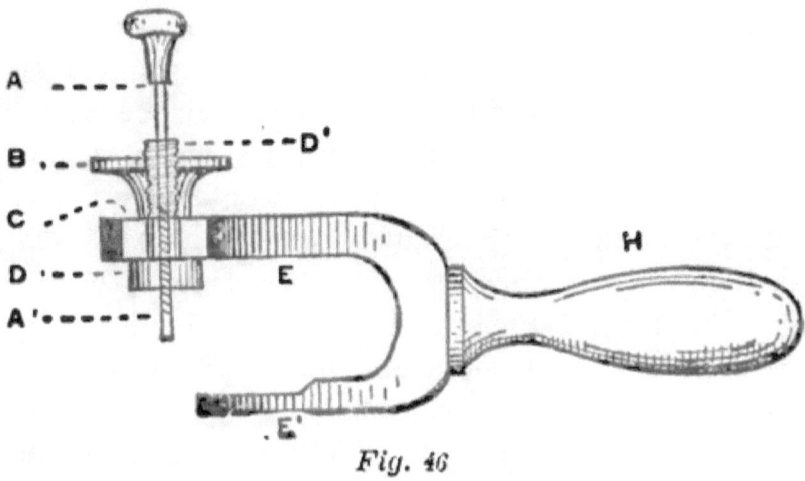

Fig. 46

too great, the arm *E'* will be too low and touch the plate; if not enough, it will be too high and touch the regulator pins. Therefore, all that is necessary to do is to move the screw *A A'* up or down as the case may be, sufficiently to ensure that the arm *E'* will assume the position the *arm of the balance* is to have. Take an 18-size balance with oversprung hairspring; the arm is at the bottom of the rim, in that case. When measuring, the screw *A'* is adjusted as to bring the arm E' close to the plate, when A' is resting on the balance jewel, if the balance is old style with undersprung hairspring, the balance arm is at top of rim, in which case A' is adjusted so that the arm E' is close to the balance cock; if the balance arm is in the center of the rim, as in some English and Swiss balances, the screw A' is adjusted so that the arm E' is midway between the plate and cock.

The reason the part A, B, D, A' is arranged to move laterally in slot C is because all balance shoulders are not the same distance from the center, and where, in some cases, the screw A' would be in a line with the center of the staff when the arm E' was resting on the balance seat, in other cases it would reach past the center, of course, short of it; and, therefore, it is made adjustable to suit all cases.

Douzieme. A measuring tool having two limbs hinged together similar to a pair of scissors. One of the limbs terminates in a pointer that indicates upon a scale the extent to which the jaws are opened. The true Douzieme gauge has a scale divided into twelfths, though some patterns are now made that have a scale divided into tenths and hundreds of an inch, and again there are others that measure the fractions of a millimeter. This tool is useful for taking measurements of all kinds. For example, we will suppose that the watchmaker is

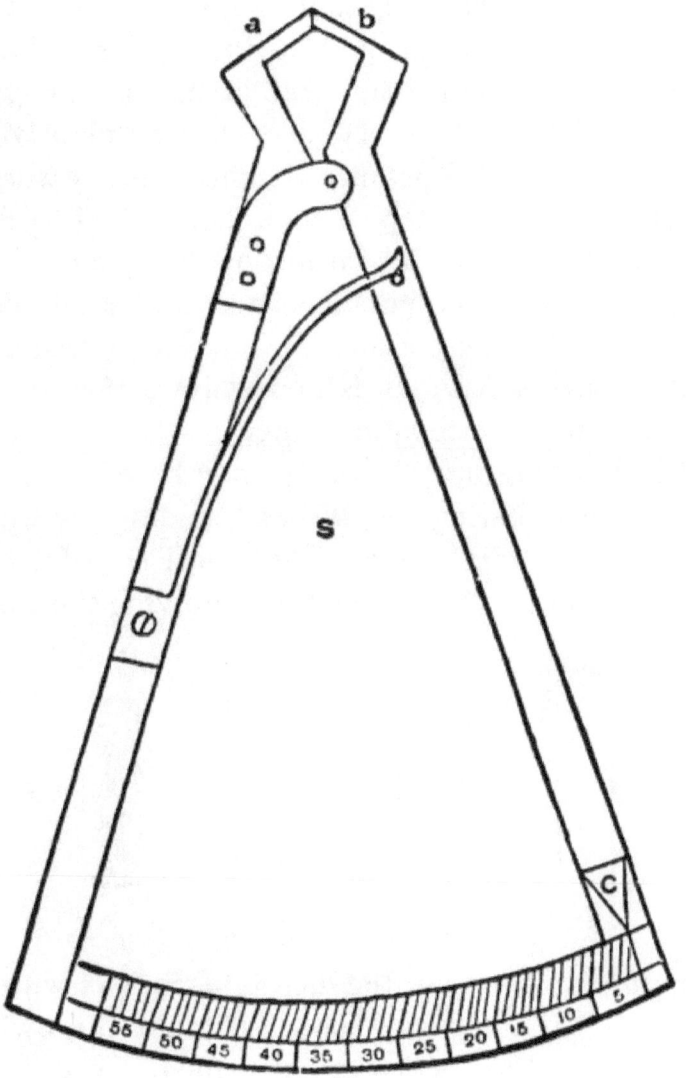

Fig. 47.

putting in a new balance staff; we will take it for granted that the upper part of the staff is entirely finished and that he is ready to find the total length that the staff should be. He takes the top plate with the balance cock and potance attached, and measures the distance from the top of cock hole jewel to top of potance hole jewel by means of this gauge. He places the jaw *a* on potance jewel and *b* on cock jewel, and notes the number on the scale that the pointer is opposite, which is generally 30 for an 18 size full plate American movement.

Drills and Drilling. Drilling may be effected in two ways, by rotating the drill and holding the work stationary, or *vice versa*. The most satisfactory results, however, are obtained by revolving the work

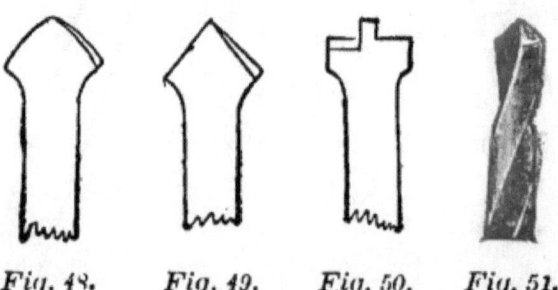

Fig. 48.   Fig. 49.   Fig. 50.   Fig. 51.

and gradually bringing the drill into contact with it. Although it is not always possible to do this, owing to the shape of the article to be drilled. A drill of the shape shown in Fig. 48 is preferable for drilling hardened steel, while the shape shown in Fig. 49 is best suited for drilling soft steel, brass, etc. Oil or glycerine diluted with alcohol, is the best lubricant for the softer metals, but when drilling hard steel turpentine should be used. Drills of the form shown in Fig. 50 are used for drilling flat bottomed holes, for countersinking screw heads, etc. The twist drill shown in Fig. 51 is desirable when drilling deeply, as this form of drill heats slowly and the particles are carried to the surface of the work. Pivot drills, like those shown in Fig. 52, can be purchased from material dealers, mounted on cards, and ready for use at such small cost that it will scarcely pay the watchmakers to make them.

Fig. 52.

Drills of a form indicated by Fig. 53, are recommended highly by Saunier, and are known as semi-cylindrical drills. They are made from cylindrical steel rods, rounded at their ends and filed down to a trifle less than half their thickness. The length of the point should be greater or less according to the nature of the metal to be operated upon, but under no circumstances must the point itself be sharp. This form of drill should be sharpened

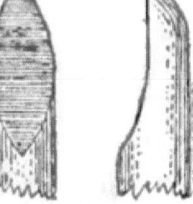

Fig. 53.

on the round side and not on the flat surface. It possesses, says Saunier, the advantage that when placed in a drill-chuck it can be turned exactly round, of the required diameter and finished; so that whenever replaced in the chuck, one can be certain beforehand that the hole drilled will be of a definite diameter. With such a drill the hole is smoothed immediately after it is made by one or the other cutting edges.

PART VI.

PRACTICAL RECEIPTS.

Gold Springs. To impart the requisite degree of elasticity to gold detent and balance springs, they should be enclosed in suitable sized steel tubes, having close fitting covers, and the tubes heated over an alcohol lamp until the steel is of a blue temper. Remove at this point from the flame and allow the whole to cool slowly. In the case of balance springs, they should be first coiled upon a block before inserting in the tube.

To Soften a Spring. A spring may be laid flat and its temper drawn between two plates fastened together by a screw through the center, and placed upon the annealing plate. A small piece of whitened steel is laid upon it, to enable the operator to judge of the degree of heat. Before opening, let it cool. When drawing the temper lay the coils farther apart.

Relation of Main Spring to Barrel. If we wish to have a mainspring theoretically adjusted, there is no better method than simply to allow one third empty space, one-third for the barrel arbor and the remainder for the spring. When a spring is at rest on the barrel, at either side of the arbor it should occupy one-sixth of the barrel's inside diameter. If we divide a barrel into sixty equal parts, we shall always see the barrel arbor is just twenty of these parts. It is a great mistake to have a barrel arbor too small, for when such is the case it is almost sure to break the mainspring if the center is at all stubborn, as is very often the case with the cheap class of mainsprings in the market.

To Prevent Rusty Hairsprings. Brush the outside of the paper parcel, containing the springs, with olive oil, a small quantity only

To Remove Stains from Watch Dials. To remove black or cloudy stains from porcelain watch dials, which are generally caused by the tin boxes they are shipped in, wet a piece of tissue paper in nitric acid and wipe the dial. This will instantly remove them. After applying the acid the dial should be immediately washed thoroughly in water and then be dried in boxwood sawdust.

To Remove Name from Dial. Take a little diamond powder made into a paste with fine oil, on the upper end of a copper polisher, the surface of which has been freshly filed and slightly rounded. On rubbing the marks they will be seen to rapidly disappear. The surface is left a little dull; it may be rendered bright by rubbing with the same powder mixed with a greater quantity of oil, and applied with a stick of pegwood. Operators will do well to previously experiment with several degrees of fineness of the powder on old dials.

To Drill Enamel Dials. You may have to drill or broach holes in enamel dials. For this purpose use a flat ended drill or conical broach of copper, into which diamond powder has been hammered. A graver kept moistened with turpentine is sometimes used. The edges of the holes in dials may be trimmed with corundum sticks, to be obtained at material shops.

To Whiten Silver Watch Dials. Flatten a piece of charcoal by rubbing it on a flat stone; on this place the dial, face upward; apply a gentle heat carefully with a blowpipe, allowing the flame to play all over the surface of the dial without touching it, so as to thoroughly heat without warping the dial. Then pickle and rinse, using acid enough to make the water very tart, immersing but for a few seconds. Silver watch dials may also be annealed by heating them red hot on a flat piece of copper over a clear fire.

Fitting the Hands. If the body of the canon pinion will not bear turning in fitting it to the hour wheel, the hour wheel should be opened in the mandrel, as it cannot be kept true by opening the hole in the fingers. Fitting the hands to a watch deserves more care and attention than are generally given to it.

The way hands are commonly fitted to watches is bad in principle. The pipe of the hour wheel is left too long, and that of the minute hand too short, and when the end shake of the hour hand is adjusted, as it usually is, lay the boss on the hour wheel and the dial, and the end shake of the center wheel affects it, sometimes giving it too much and bending the hour hand by its catching the minute hand either in setting the hands or in the going of the watch. In fitting the hands, the examiner should fit the glass, ir to a hunting case, as high as the case will admit, ascertain the space available by placing a piece or beeswax on the dial and pressing the glass down on it, and turn the canon pinion until it projects from the dial the height of the beeswax; the hour wheel pipe should rise just perceptibly above the dial, and the end shake of the hour hand be adjusted by the the pipe of the minute hand and that of the hour wheel.

Reducing Diameter of a Watch Glass. The diameter of a watch glass can be reduced by centering in a lathe, chucking it between two pieces of cork, or a pair of cork arbors, and applying a moistened piece of glass to the edge, or an emery stick. When the desired diameter is attained, polish the edge with pumice stone, followed by putty powder applied on a wet cork.

The Functions of Oil Sinks. Oil sinks are formed in watch and clock plates so that, by capillary attraction, the oil is kept close to the pivot instead of spreading over the plate; and back slopes are formed on the arbors so that the oil may not be drawn all up the body of the arbor. The "attraction" is sometimes negative and becomes a repulsion, as is the case with mercury in a glass tube. It is still called capillary, whether the fluid is raised above its natural level or depressed below it.

Cutting Screw Threads. It is quite a knack to make a nice screw, and beginners are generally apt to use too much force when cutting the thread. If the spindle has been turned too large for the hole in the screw-plate there is danger of breaking the screw-plate, if it is over hard, and pieces will chip off; again, the piece to be tapped is apt to break and stop up the hole in the plate, thereby entailing the tedious job of drilling the piece out and cleaning the thread. It is better to begin with a hole much too large and work down gradually. It is natural that a certain amount of force must be employed, and a little practice will soon teach the beginner how much to insure a full, good thread. Now, put the screw back in the lathe, and turn the head a little more than the the required thickness, and cut the screw off by turning a groove out.

To Remove Broken Screws. Any one having an American lathe can, with small expense of time and labor, make a small attachment which will easily and quickly remove a broken screw from the plate or pillar of any watch.

Take two common steel watch keys having hardened and tempered pipes, size, four or five, having care that the squares in each are of the same size and of good depth. Cut off the pipes about half an inch from the end; file up one of these for about half its length, on three equal sides, to fit one of the large split chucks of the lathe. Drill a hole in one of the brass centers of the lathe of sufficient size and depth, into which insert the other key-pipe, and fasten with a little soft solder. Soften a piece of Stubs wire, to work easily in the lathe, and turn down an eighth of an inch from the end to a size a little smaller than the broken screw in the plate; finish with a conical shoulder, for greater strength, and cross-file the end with a fine slot or knife-edge file, that the tool may not slip on the end of the broken screw; cut off the wire a half inch from the end, and file down to a square that will fit closely into one of the key-pipes, make a second point like the first one and fit to the other key-pipe, harden in oil, polish, and temper to a dark straw color. Fit the brass center into the tail stock. To use, put the tools in place in the lathe, place the broken end of the screw against the end of the point in the lathe head; slide up the back center and fasten the point firmly against the other end of the screw, that it may not slip or turn; revolve the plate slowly, and the broken screw, being held fast between the two points, will be quickly removed. To remove a broken pillar screw: Place the broken screw against the point in the lathe-head, holding the plate firmly with the right hand, the pillar on a line with the lathe center; turn the lathe-head slowly backward with the left hand, and the screw will be removed. Should the tool slip on the broken screw, and fail to draw it out, drill a hole in the pillar from the lower or dial side, down to the screw point (if the size of the pillar in the plate will admit of so doing), and with the second point in the back center, remove the screw in the same manner as the plate screw in the first process. Five or six sizes of these points will be found sufficient for a majority of these breakages that may occur.

To Polish Pivots. Turn the pivots down about to size, grind with oilstone dust and oil, until the marks of the graver are removed and a smooth gray or dead-white surface is obtained; then polish with diamantine. The grinding and polishing are best done with slips of bell metal filed to shape. The polishing should not be continued too long, or the surface will become brown and of inferior appearance. If the brown shows itself, the surface should again be stoned off and the polishing repeated.

The Size of the Cylinder Pivot. The side-shake in cylinder pivot holes should be greater than that for ordinary train holes; one-sixth is about the right amount. The size of pivot relative to the cylinder should be about one-eighth the diameter of the body of the cylinder. It is very necessary that this amount of side-shake should be correctly recognized; if less than the amount stated, the watch, though performing well when the oil is fresh, fails to do so when it commences to thicken. The only accurate way of getting at the correct amount of shake is to fit a pivot or two to a jewel hole by means of a micrometer; the eye will soon become capable of correctly ascertaining the amount necessary. If any doubt exists, a round broach can be used to size the pivot hole, and the micometer will then decide the question.

Shape of Pivots. Pivots must be hard, round and well polished; their shoulders are to be flat, not too large, with ends rounded slightly off so that they do not wear the cap jewel. The jewel holes must be round, smooth and not larger than is requisite for the free motion of the pivot which is surrounded with oil. Their sides must be parallel to those of the pivots, so that they sustain the pressure of the pivot equally at all points of their length. The holes, if of brass or gold, must have been hammered sufficiently hard so that the pores of the metal are closed to prevent too rapid wear. It is well if the oil sinks are of a size that will accommodate a sufficient quantity of oil, which, if too little, would soon dry out or become thickened with the worn-off particles of the metal. The under turnings of the pinion leaves are conical, but in such a way that the thicker part be nearest to the pivot, because by this disposition the oil is retained at the pivot by attraction, and does not seek to spread into the pinion leaves, as is often the case, especially with flat watches in which this provision is frequently slighted.

Friction of the Train Pivots. It is very important to reduce the friction of the wheel pivots to a minimum quantity, and to make it constant so that the motive power be transmitted with the greatest possible uniformity to the pendulum, which is necessary to enable the latter to maintain its arc of oscillation of the same magnitude. The friction of the pivots is due to the pressure of the motive power and the weight of the wheels. The wheel work nearest the motive power must have strong pivots so that they possess sufficient resistence, neither wear the pivot holes to one side nor enlarge them, by which the friction would be increased and at the same time alter the true point of engagement. In tenor with the distance of the wheels from the motive power, the thicknesses of their pivots must decrease because these latter sustain less pressure, and are subject to a greater velocity than the first parts.

To Fit a Bushing. After repairing the pivot, a bush is selected as small as the pivot will admit. Open the hole of the plate or cock so that the bush, (which previously should be lightly draw-filed at the end), will stand with a slight pressure upright in the opened hole of the plate or cock; then, with a knife, cut it across at the part where it is to be broken off so that it may break very readily when required to do so. Press it in the plate on the side the pivot works, break off, and then drive it home with a small center punch. In every repair of this nature, notice should be taken of the amount of end shake of the pinion, and allowance made by leaving the bush so that any excess may be corrected. To finish off the shoulder end, a small champfering tool should be used. It has a hole smaller than the pivot one to receive a fine brass wire, serving as a center to prevent the tool from changing its position while being used; or the wire may be put through the bush holes, and the hole of the tool may be left open. The above is a far more expeditious way than using the lathe.

To Measure Length of Staff. The proper way to measure for the length of staff is, first, to take off both end stones, fit the balance cock properly to the plate (level, etc.), and screw it fast in its place. Then, with the degree gauge, take the measure from the outside of one hole jewel to the outside of the other one and to this add the amount of end shake the staff is to have, which gives the exact length of the staff between the extreme ends of the pivots. The length should be such that when one pivot rests against its end stone the top pivot shall come level with the outer surface of its hole jewel, and the same when resting on the other pivot. The end shake should be equal to the distance from the outer surface of the hole jewel to the adjacent surface of its end stone when fastened in place. If this distance is neither too great or small (the jewels must not touch), the end shake will be correct. A safe way for length is to take the outside measure from the surface of the sink in which the bottom end stone fitting rests, to the top surface of the balance cock. Then, having screwed on one of the end stones, shorten up either or both pivots of the finished staff a trifle, to bring the top end of the other pivot level with the surface of its hole jewel as before explained.

Pinion Diameter. The following are excellent rules for determining the correct diameter of a pinion by measuring teeth of the wheel that sizes into it. The term *full*, used below, indicates full measure from outside to outside of the teeth named, and the term *center* the measure from the center of one tooth to the center of the other tooth named, inclusive. For diameter of a pinion of 15 leaves measure, with calipers, a shade less than 6 teeth of the wheel center. For diameter of a pinion of 12 leaves measure with calipers, 5 teeth of the wheel, center. For diameter of a pinion of 10 leaves measure, with calipers 4 teeth of the wheel, full. For diameter of a pinion of 9 leaves measure, with calipers, a little less than 4 teeth of the wheel, full. For diameter of a pinion of 8 leaves measure, with calipers, a little less than 4 teeth of the wheel, center. For diameter of a pinion of 7 leaves measure, with calipers, a little less than 3 teeth of the wheel, full. For diameter of a pinion of 6 leaves measure, with calipers, 3 teeth of the wheel, center. For diameter of a pinion of 5 leaves measure, with calipers, 3 teeth of the wheel, center. As a general rule, pinions that lead, as in the hour wheel, should be somewhat larger than those that drive, and pinions of clocks should generally be somewhat larger proportionally than those of watches.

To Anneal a Staff or Pinion. It sometimes becomes necessary to anneal a staff or pinion, in which you wish to insert a pivot, without removing it from the wheel. To do this, place the whole part or end of the staff or pinion in a pin-vise or sliding-tongs, which, of course, is cold; now pierce the top of a brass thimble, so that the end to be drilled will go in snug; then, with a blow-pipe and small spirit lamp throw as much heat as you wish on the article to be drilled, by blowing directly into the thimble, without in the least heating the wheel.

To Remedy Worn Pinions. Turn the leaves or rollers so that the worn places upon them will be toward the arbor or shaft and fasten them in that position. If they are "rolling pinions," and cannot be secured otherwise, it will be better to do it with a little soft solder.

To Tighten a Canon Pinion. The canon pinion is sometimes too loose upon the center arbor. Grasp the arbor lightly with a pair of cutting nippers, and by a single turn of the nippers around the arbor, cut or raise a small thread thereon.

To Remove Rust. The best way to remove rust from pinions is to scour them up with oil-stone dust and oil, until a smooth surface is obtained, then polish them with crocus. Care must be taken not to grind the leaves off any more than is necessary, or the proper shape may be destroyed. Some workmen soak the rusted parts in a solution of cyanide of potassium or other solvent of oxide of iron, but the use of such means cannot be approved of. The way described is as good as any, and is safe. If the pinions are very badly rusted they should be rejected and others put in, as they will be out of shape when finished off smooth, and would not perform well in the watch.

Putting Teeth into Wheels. To put in teeth in watch or clock wheels without dovetailing or soldering them, drill a hole somewhat wider than the tooth square through the plate, a little below the tooth. Cut from the edge of the wheel, square down to the hole already drilled; then flatten a piece of wire so as to fit snugly into the cut of the saw, and with a light hammer form a head on it like the head of a pin. When thus prepared, press the wire or pin into the empty space of the wheel, the head filling the hole drilled through the plate, and then projecting out so as to form the tooth; then with a sharp pointed graver cut a small groove each side of the pin from the edge of the wheel down to the hole, and with a blow of your hammer spread the face of the pin so as to fill the groove just cut. Repeat the same operation on the other side of the wheel and finish off in the usual way. The tooth will be found perfectly riveted in on every side and as strong as the original one, while in appearance it will be equal to the best dovetailed job.

To Polish a Watch Wheel. It can be done nicely in the following manner: get a cork, flat on the top, and put into a vice; on it place the wheel, as far as the pinion will allow; then take a bluestone and water and grind the wheel smooth and flat, all the time revolving it with the left hand; wash it, and put in a box with some slacked powdered lime. This is done simply for the purpose of drying it, and preventing the pinion from getting stained or rusty. Brush it out nice and clean, put another cork, clean and flat, in the vice, and pound some crocus on a stake. Some workmen add a little rouge, but this is simply a matter of taste. Take a slip of tin, about the size of a watchmaker's file, only thicker, file the end of one side flat and smooth, charge it with a little of the crocus, and polish the wheel, all the time rotating it with your left hand; do not cease until both wheel and tin polisher are almost dry, so that you can see the polish, when, if to your satisfaction, clean the wheel off with a piece of soft bread, and brush it out. Should it be scratched, bread it off, clean off the tin, and take a new supply of crocus. Cleanliness in this manipulation is of the greatest importance, for if there should be any grit about the crocus, polisher, or the fingers of the workman, the work will be full of scratches. This applies simply to bar wheels.

To Bush a Wheel. A watch will frequently stop because a wheel is improperly centered in itself, whereby one side will gear too deep, the other too shallow, into the pinion driven by it. Such a wheel likely is of the proper size and has good teeth, but the difficulty is its proper centering, when fitted to its pinion. The following will be found to be an easy way of correction. Take a piece of lead of about the thickness of a silver half dollar, and clip and file it round so that it will fit into one of the larger steps in a step chuck of an American lathe. Screw it fast into the lathe, and while revolving, center and drill a hole of about the size of a winding arbor. Then, with a graver, turn out a recess, the size and a trifle more than the thickness of the wheel, so that it will fit in exact, with its teeth touching the outside of the cut. Drive the wheel from its pinion, and broach out the center, so as to take a bush of sufficient length, which should be firmly riveted in and filed smooth on the lower side. Turn a small groove around the outside of the cut in the lead, crowd in the wheel, with a burnisher set as a gavel. This fixes the wheel perfectly true on the outside. Now center and drill, leaving a little to be turned and with a fine polished graver, to fit the same pinion. Rivet on, and your wheel is all right.

To Grind Down Plates or Wheels. The stoning down of plates or wheels with emery or bluestone is rather a tedious job, especially for him who has much of it to do. It can be made easier, however, by using a little soap. The work is more rapidly performed and finer stoning is obtained.

To Test the Quality of Watch Jewels. Place the jewel on a piece of charcoal, and with the blow pipe and spirit lamp bring it to a bright cherry red. If the stone is perfect and of the proper density, the heat will not effect it; otherwise, the heat will bring out the imperfections, which can easily be detected with a double lens glass. To ascertain if a jewel hole is perfectly polished, place a piece of white paper on your work board and hold the jeweled plate about two inches above the paper and parallel to it, so as to allow the light to pass between the plate and the paper; shade the jewel with a small ring to prevent the light from reflecting from the top of the stone, and with your double lens glass look straight through the jewel hole to the paper. If it is perfectly polished it will appear to have a fine black ring around the inside of the hole. If the jewel is a ruby or a garnet, use black paper instead of white.

Replace a Broken Foot Jewel. Remove the broken jewel from the collet or setting; place the collet or setting in one of your lathe chucks, large enough to hold the same; start in motion, and with a fine pointed burnisher raise the bezel sufficient to receive a new jewel; select a jewel to fit both pivot and setting, replace in chuck, and with a little larger burnisher close down the bezel on jewel, and your job is complete.

Tightening Ruby Pins. If it is necessary to tighten a ruby pin, set it in asphaltum varnish. It will become hard in a few minutes, and be much firmer and better than in shellac, as generally used.

To Polish Jewel Settings. A very good way to polish jewel settings to American watches, of brass or gold, is as follows: First turn the setting down to the right thickness, or nearly so, and then grind down to a gray on a ground glass slab with rotten stone, then clean off the oily rotten stone and polish on a boxwood lap with diamantine and oil, which gives a nice gloss. It will also give a nice gloss on steel, only use oil stone to gray steel with, instead of rotten stone. The operator should be particular to clean off all the graying powder in each case before using the boxwood lap, and be sure to keep the lap in a place free from grit or dust when not in use; brass watch wheels can be finished in the same way as the jewel settings by the same process.

New Jewels. The bad action of a watch may frequently be traced to imperfect jewels. The repairer should carefully examine every jewel in a watch taken down for repairs, and if he finds one with the hole too large, or "out of round," that is, much wider in one direction than in another, it should be replaced by a good one, in the following manner: If the depth is correct, notice whether the jewel is above or below the surface of the plate; if it is either, then knock it out and cement the plate or bridge on a chuck in the lathe, being careful to get it on true, by the hole lately occupied by the jewel. By means of a burnisher raise the burr that holds the jewel in, and if a jewel can be found of the proper size and thickness, and the hole not too large, it can readily be "rubbed in" with the burnisher; if the hole is too small, it can be opened. The chuck on which the article is cemented should have a hole from a quarter to a half an inch deep in its centre. If no jewels can be found of the right size and thickness, select one a little too large, enlarge the hole sufficiently to put the jewel in, and then proceed to fasten it. If the jewel is broken, of course the same remarks apply to replacing it with a good one. One difficulty that the watchmaker has to contend with, in selecting a jewel from the indifferent lot supplied by some dealers, is to find one, the hole of which is in the center of the jewel. If a jewel is not true, or rather, if the hole in it is not in the center, it must be cemented into a chuck in the lathe, trued up by the hole, then turned off with a diamond cutter, and the chamfer carefully trued up and polished again; while in the lathe it can be turned down to fit the hole in the setting. The shellac is to be removed from the plate with alcohol. In many instances a chuck will have to be turned up to suit the particular job to be done. Care must be taken in opening, or the jewel will break or chip around the hole. The corners must be carefully rounded by a piece of wire larger than the hole, the end of which is conical. It will take but a moment to do this, but if care is not taken too much will be taken off.

To Mark Tools. Cover the part to be marked with a thin coating of tallow and beeswax; with a sharp instrument write the name in the tallow, cutting clearly into it; fill the letters with nitric acid, and let it remain from one to ten minutes; dip in water and rub off, and you have the mark etched.

The Rose Cutter. The rose cutter is quite a valuable adjunct to a lathe, and is fixed to the spindle in the same manner as a chuck, and will be found exceedingly useful for quickly reducing pieces of wire for screws, etc., to a gauge. For screws, the wire should be of a proper size for the screw

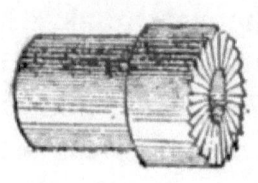

Fig. 54.

heads, and a cutter selected with a hole the size of the finished screw. The point of the wire is rounded to enter the hole of the cutter, against which it is forced by the back center of the lathe, the serrated face of the cutter rapidly cutting away the superfluous metal, the part intended for the screw passes into the hole in the cutter. Some care is required in rounding the point of the wire, for if not done equally all around, the screw will not be true to the head.

To Prepare Chalk. Pulverize the chalk thoroughly and then mix it with clean rain water, in proportions of two pounds to the gallon. Stir well, and then let it stand about two minutes. In this time the gritty matter will have settled to the bottom. Slowly pour the water into another vessel, so as not to stir up the sediment. Let stand until entirely settled, and then pour off as before. The settlings in the second vessel will be prepared chalk, ready for use as soon as dried. Spanish whiting, treated in the same way, makes a very good cleaning or polishing powder. Some watchmakers add a little crocus, and we think it an improvement; it gives the powder a nice color, at least, and therefore adds to its importance in the eyes of the uninitiated.

To Remove Finger Marks on Gilt Clocks. Dissolve cyanide of potassium, ¼ oz. in ½ pint of water; paint the mark with the solution, then scratch-brush, finish with washing in hot water.

Sweating of Show Windows. Take one-fourth pound glycerine to two and one-fourth quarts alcohol, and a little essential oil; the quantity of glycerine varies according to its quality. By the composition of the above specified ingredients, the essential oil is dissolved by the alcohol, and the fluid united with the glycerine. It may be done at ordinary temperature, and it is not necessary to expose the mixture to heat. This is applied to the inside of the window. The pane is either rubbed with a clean linen cloth, or else the fluid mass is applied with a camel's hair brush, and the blind appearance of the glass, owing to overheating, is entirely overcome.

To Remove Ink Stains from Silver. Silver pen holders and ink-stands frequently become deeply discolored with ink, and the stains are sometimes very difficult to remove. They may be removed by rubbing the stains with a paste composed of chloride of lime and water.

To Clean Watch Cases. Very dirty or oxidized silver or gold watch cases can be restored by brushing them with a soft brush and a little rouge and oil. The case is afterward cleaned with another brush and a little (best is lukewarm) water and soap, and finally laid in alcohol to remove all traces of the soap. The case after being taken from the alcohol, is dried with a clean rag. It is evident that the movement and, if possible, the case springs, have been taken out. Clean dry sawdust may be used in place of alcohol; leave the case in it until thoroughly dry.

To Remove Stains from Marble Cases. To remove stains from marble cases, clock dials, etc., take equal parts of fresh oil of vitriol and lemon juice; shake up these substances very thoroughly in a bottle, wet spot with the mixture, and in a few minutes afterward rub with a soft linen cloth and the spots will be found to have disappeared.

To Drill into Hard Steel. Make your drill oval in form, instead of the usual pointed shape, and temper as hard as it will bear without breaking; then roughen the surface which you desire to drill with a little diluted muriatic acid, and, instead of oil, use turpentine or glycerine, in which a little gum camphor has been dissolved, as a lubricant. In operating, keep the pressure on your drill firm and steady; and if the bottom of the hole should chance to become burnished, so the drill will not act, as sometimes happens, again roughen with diluted acid as before; then clean out the hole carefully and proceed again.

To Temper Drills. Select none but the finest and best steel for your drills. In making them, never heat higher than a cherry red, and always hammer till nearly cold. Do all your hammering in one way, for if, after you have flattened out your piece, you attempt to hammer it back to a square or round, you will ruin it. When your drill is in proper shape, heat it to a cherry red and thrust it into a piece of resin or into mercury. Some use a solution of cyanuret of potassia and rain water for tempering their drills, but the resin or mercury will give better results.

To Drill Pearls. The easiest way to hold pearls, in order to drill and otherwise cut them, is to fit them loosely in holes bored in a piece of wood. A few drops of water sprinkled about the holes causes the wood fibres to swell and hold the pearls firmly. When the wood dries they fall out.

To Clean Pearls. Soak them in warm water in which bran has been boiled, with a little salts of tartar and alum, rubbing gently between the hands. When the water is cold, renew the operation until the discoloration is removed; rinse in luke warm water, and lay the pearls in white paper in a dark place to cool and dry.

To Renovate Bronze. Bronze may be renovated and re-colored by mixing one part of muriatic acid and two parts of water. Free the article from all grease and dirt and apply the acid with a cloth. When dry polish it with beeswax or sweet oil.

To Separate Silver from Copper. Mix sulphuric acid, 1 part; nitric acid, 1 part; water, 1 part. Boil the metal in the mixture until it dissolves, then throw in a little salt, which will cause the silver to deposit.

To Frost Watch Caps and Plates. Take two and one-half parts nitric acid, and two parts muriatic acid, full strength. Dip in the articles for a few seconds, rinse in clear water, scratch brush with a circular motion, then gild.

To Frost Watch Plates. Watch plates are frosted by means of fine brass wire scratch brushes fixed in a lathe, and made to revolve at great speed, the end of the wire brushes striking the plate producing a beautiful appearance; or, sink that part of the movement to be frosted for a short time into a mixture of nitric acid, muriatic acid and table salt, one ounce of each. On removing from the acid, place it in a shallow vessel containing enough sour beer to nearly cover it, then with a fine scratch brush scour thoroughly, letting it remain under the beer during the operation. Then wash off, first in pure water and then in alcohol. Gild or silver in accordance with any receipt.

To Take Spots off Gilding. Boil common alum in soft, pure water and immerse the article in the solution, or rub the spot with it and dry with sawdust.

Imitation Patina. Mix carbonate of copper and any light alcoholic varnish and apply to the object with a brush. This paint will penetrate the smallest recesses of bronze objects, and when dry has the appearance of patina. Carbonate of copper gives a blue patina, vertigris a light green and intermediate shades may be produced by mixing the two.

www.ingramcontent.com/pod-product-compliance
Lightning Source LLC
Chambersburg PA
CBHW030905170426
43193CB00009BA/735

*9 7 8 3 3 3 7 1 3 8 0 2 8 *